ANOTHER
KIND
OF
LOVE
Homosexuality and Spirituality

Practical . . . Valuable . . . Compassionate

"One witness to the positive role [the homosexual community can play] can be found in *Another Kind of Love*. . . . the book will prove valuable to anyone interested in a spiritual understanding of homosexuality . . . Woods shows sensitivity to the worst as well as the best aspects of the homosexual subculture in the United States today . . . This book offers one of the best-informed and pastorally sensitive messages of joy and hope yet to be published."

—John J. McNeill in *America*

"Based on experience as a member of a team ministering to homosexuals, the author writes for homosexual men and women, their relatives and friends, and others who care, exploring the practical, pastoral and spiritual implications and problems of homosexuals."—*Catholic Library World*

"[This] is a difficult subject, but Woods handles it with great understanding and compassion. His discussion of the fourteen sexes is outstanding, since he points out that 'male and female' are two very general concepts . . . His caring, Christian approach to this difficult topic and his pastoral approach to the subject make it easy to recommend this book as one of the best in this field in recent years."—*The Priest*

"To say the least, the book is an eye-opener because it deals with one of the most maligned and least understood phenomena of all time . . . It is not a theological study—but it frankly explores the practical, pastoral and spiritual implications, and sometimes problems, involved in the factual, lived situations of Christian men and women whose sexual orientation extends to members of their own sex . . . You may not agree with every contention that the author makes throughout the book, but coming from a priest who has ministered to the gay community for six years, it will certainly give you a better understanding of what homosexuality is, and it will make you more sympathetic . . ."—*The Church World*

"Woods is not another John McNeill, but he does manage to effectively communicate the spiritual quality of the loving gay relationship."—*Bay Area Reporter*

"In [a] wilderness of negativism it was quite refreshing to read *Another Kind of Love* . . . Woods presents a fresh and positive approach to living the gay life, especially from the Christian viewpoint . . . Since the Church, in all her various forms, has offered no positive view of homosexuality and the gay life, for the gay Christian, Father Woods' treatment of the gay's spiritual life is especially valuable."—*GPU News*

"Parts of this book are outstanding in their quality of compassion and human sensitivity. The overall spiritual tone of the work comes from a quest for meaning in quiet suffering. Anyone would benefit from the book's evocation of openness which can risk pain and anxiety for a higher good . . . Father Woods does a great service by appealing to gay persons to cooperate with researchers in yielding new perspectives on gayness . . . I thank him for his efforts."

—*Marriage & Family Living*

ANOTHER KIND OF LOVE

*Homosexuality
and
Spirituality*

Richard Woods

IMAGE BOOKS
A Division of Doubleday & Company, Inc.
Garden City, New York
1978

Image Book edition published September, 1978 by special arrangement with the Thomas More Association

Copyright © 1978 by Richard Woods
Copyright © 1977 by the Thomas More Association. All rights reserved. Printed in the United States of America.

ISBN: 0-385-14312-5
Library of Congress Catalog Card Number: 77-27729

CONTENTS

INTRODUCTION TO THE IMAGE EDITION

When this book appeared, it evoked "widespread critical reaction," as the saying goes. Not that there were many notices. Some were very brief. Rather, the *range* of response was extensive—from warm endorsement to icy horror. It was dismissed as both outrageous and naïve, and it was welcomed as a balanced treatment of a highly controversial issue. In short, and not surprisingly, the reviews were a mixed bag.

Shortly after the book was published, I also began receiving personal letters. The over-all message of the ordinary men and women for whom the book had been written was modest and simple. In effect, they said "Thanks." Somewhat surprisingly, I received only one unfavorable letter.

The invitation to prepare a revised edition for Image Books was therefore doubly welcome. For it gave me the opportunity to profit from the critical reviews and to reach a wider audience. Although the text remains largely unchanged, I have added some new material—most notably the chapter on spirituality. I have also attempted to remedy the weakness of the first edition with regard to gay women, about whose lives and experience we are only slowly gaining the kind of information and insight which even in the case of gay men is still scant and episodic.

Adding this "concluding untheological postscript" also provides me with the opportunity to reflect briefly on some of the issues connected with the book a year after its initial appearance.

When Joel Wells invited me to write the book, it was intended for the Thomas More Press "Living with" series. The eventual decision to change the format and the title to *Another Kind of Love* bothered me at first, because it seemed to oppose homosexual love to heterosexual love. I felt that what was essential about human love applied both to gay and straight persons, and to men and women. Eventually, however, I became more comfortable with the change. I am still convinced that all human love is fundamentally the same, that gay men and women are above all human, and that their lives and loving are no different from those of anyone else. However, the situation and thus the experience of gay persons are significantly different from those of straight people *within* the common human condition. It is important to acknowledge those differences as well as the common elements of experience—and that is what the title in fact suggests.

Several objections have been lodged against the subtitle, which was my doing, mainly to the effect that I nowhere treated spirituality directly. This observation is valid. As "an essay *in* spirituality," not *about* it, I intended the book as a whole to reflect the spirituality of gay men and women. The chapter originally entitled "Gay Spirituality" was to that extent misleading—especially because the last *four* chapters were an effort to explore various dimensions of that spirituality.

A gay spirituality, like those of other special groups of Christians, is latent in the fundamental experience of gay life itself. But these implicit elements and a structure with which to integrate them have yet to be explicitly articulated. No one person will be able to achieve that task for the simple reason that spirituality is both pluralistic and social. There are not only many dimensions of spirituality, there are many spiritualities latent in the gay world, and the process of explicating them will be a collective one. To that end, I have added a chapter which represents one of a number of possible ways of approaching that task.

My discussion of language also aroused some dissidence, especially in the gay press. Two topics seem to warrant some attention here—first, the use of the words "gay" and "Lesbian," and, second, the issue of cross-gender references as a form of camp.

The demand by some militant Lesbians that "gay" be restricted to males, while an understandable position in terms of the need for greater visibility among women in the gay world (and the straight world), is, I am convinced, self-defeating. For one thing, "gay" customarily refers to both men and women, and in fact may have originally referred mainly to women. For another, there are enough real tensions and divisions in the gay world without adding artificial ones. Further, "gay" signifies consciousness, not gender. It thus functions as a unifying term, as in "gay liberation," avoiding the sexist implications of a world already too embroiled in gender conflicts. If Lesbians are overlooked in the gay world and in books such as this one, torturing the language and widening the rift between gay men and women will only worsen the situation.

The second issue concerns gender-crossing camp. Blacks can call each other "nigger" without inciting a riot, gay men can call each other "faggot" without offense, even though in both cases mild irony or some kind of affectionate criticism is being conveyed. In our society, however, to refer to a man—*any* man—in feminine terms is a put-down which reflects one of the ugliest facets of our male-dominated, deeply insecure culture. The inability of many gay men to grasp this is itself a symptom of how deeply embedded sexist bias is in all segments of modern life.

Here I would direct attention to the pointed discussion in *The David Kopay Story*, in which the gay former all-star describes not merely how professional athletes humiliate and taunt each other by such references, but also the scorn and fear of women which lurks behind it.[1] The ratification by gay men of such prejudicial use of feminine references in the straight world is not merely a capitulation to the same macho bias that despises "queers." It no less manifests at least an ambivalent attitude toward women—gay as well as straight. It is profoundly insensitive and may well betray a deep fear of and hostility toward women which *is* pathological.

As Del Martin and Phyllis Lyon point out in *Lesbian/ Woman*, a belief in the inferior status of women even found

[1] By David Kopay and Perry Deane Young, New York: Bantam Books ed., 1977, pp. 52–55.

expression in Lesbian culture itself in the form of an exaggerated masculine appearance and life-style affected by some women.[2] The women's liberation movement has brought about a decline in such symbolic self-depreciation by Lesbians. But male gays have somewhat further yet to go. Removing sexist language from scripture and theology, as was recommended at a recent Dignity International Convention, will be a pointless gesture if an effort is not also made—and perhaps *first* made—to remove such verbal abuse from the gay world itself.

Another sharp criticism concerned the shortness of the "shrift" I gave Lesbians in general. Admittedly, there was no chapter devoted to Lesbian experience—and still isn't. I attempted to note those facts of gay experience which pertained specifically to gay women (or didn't), but since most of my direct experience of Lesbians came through my work with Dignity, I was able to include far fewer references than are in fact warranted. For the truth is that gay women are sadly underrepresented in Dignity and similar organizations. The reasons for this, as I explained in the text, are manifold.

I have tried to lengthen the Lesbian shrift in this edition, not by adding a chapter, which would be unacceptable for several reasons—among them the unity of gay experience as distinct from the real differences between the sexes. Rather, I have enlarged those sections which were too brief and added others where appropriate without, I hope, exceeding the limits of my grasp of the Lesbian situation. I have to confess that as a man and a churchman at that, my grasp *is* deficient and will probably remain so. Consequently, the concerned critic should agitate not only for my continued education but for a thorough treatment of Lesbian experience, especially with regard to the church, from a Lesbian viewpoint.[3] Meantime, I suggest further reading from among the resources listed at the end of this book.

Finally, some comparison of this book with John McNeill's

[2] New York: Bantam Books, 1972, pp. 74–83. Lesbians are not free of gender-crossing camp, if less derogatory about it. See p. 134.

[3] For an example, see Sally Gearhart, "The Miracle of Lesbianism," in *Loving Women/Loving Men,* Sally Gearhart and William R. Johnson, eds., San Francisco: Glide Publications, 1974, pp. 118–52.

The Church and the Homosexual was inevitable. When his book was eventually released, my own manuscript was already in the hands of my publisher. Thus, despite similarities in tone and treatment, McNeill's book had no direct influence on this one, which makes our agreements perhaps more significant. But there are differences as well.

McNeill's work is a comprehensive theological statement. Mine is a pastoral essay addressed not to professional theologians or gay militants, but to ordinary Christians who may or may not be gay, but who are concerned about the gay issue as it personally touches them or someone close to them. I would also point out that McNeill's approach and mine differ with respect to the dual social system in which gay persons live, move and derive much of their self-awareness as gay. Whereas McNeill attends directly to substantial scriptural, historical and psychological issues and only tangentially with the social system, I make it the focus of concern. This is especially important, I feel, with regard to matters touching on sin and guilt which, in my opinion, cannot adequately be considered without understanding the dynamics of social structures and systems which are moral (or immoral) agencies in their own right.[4]

Much more, of course, can and will be said and written about homosexuality from a pastoral perspective. In some respects, my own views have changed from what they were when I began this book in 1976. Rather than attempt to add it all to *Another Kind of Love,* I would direct the reader's attention to the Thomas More cassette program "Gay Christians" (TM 241), in which I take up further dimensions of pastoral theology, ministry, spirituality and life-styles as they are affected by and bear upon the lives of "God's gays."

> Richard Woods, O.P.
> Oakland, California
> 25 January 1978
> Feast of the Conversion of St. Paul

[4] Cf. Patrick Kerans, *Sinful Social Structures,* New York: Paulist Press, 1974.

PRELUDE

Picking up a book on sexuality was, not too long ago, a hazardous affair for the Catholic browser; thumbing through one on homosexuality required the sheerest nerve—unless one happened to be a priest, perhaps. Times have changed. Sexuality is reasonably topical for Catholics. But, as you know by now, it is still something of a challenge to tote a book on homosexuality to the counter and present it for purchase without blushing, avoiding the salesperson's eyes, including it in a stack of other books (preferably biblical studies or psychology texts), or being a priest. Looking like a worried parent might help. Being gay might help, too.

Not many years ago, the "love that dared not speak its name" was literally unmentionable in polite conversation. Today, liberation is in the air. Many gays and lesbians are "out of the closet," proud to announce who—and what—they are. State by state, oppressive legal restrictions are being reduced. A growing movement for acceptance in the church has surfaced in the form of associations such as the Metropolitan Community Church, Dignity and Integrity. Gay men and women are interviewed on television and radio. Major films with homosexual themes are shown in neighborhood theaters. Articles and books are increasing in quantity and viewpoint.

But many, perhaps most gay men and women are still jeopardized by their orientation in the eyes of the state and the church. Many are persecuted indirectly, others are prosecuted. Many are troubled by a sense of guilt or rejection, isolated from family and religion by their sexuality. Not a few live in quiet but constant fear of exposure, ridicule and condemnation.

This book is not so much about homosexuality as it is for

homosexual men and women, especially those who are *not* "out." It is also for their relatives, friends and associates—people who care about gays, whether as teachers, pastors, co-workers or just neighbors. It is also for the curious, ambivalent, fearful and hostile—if only as a tender of hope and an invitation to care. Further, this is not a book on the psychology or sociology of sexuality, although I have not hesitated to plunder the sciences for information.

In the following pages, I intend to approach homosexuality foremost as a fact, rather than as an undesirable or desirable situation. However, I do not believe that homosexual preference as such constitutes individual or social pathology. On the whole, I have found most homosexual persons to be about as healthy (and unhealthy) as most heterosexual persons, even given the greater stress gay people must endure daily.

Finally, this is not a theological study, although theological reflection is greatly needed, and I have not resisted the temptation completely. I am particularly not concerned here with arguing theoretical problems in the area of moral theology, although they are entailed and some will be pointed out. Rather, I am concerned to explore the practical, pastoral and spiritual implications and sometimes problems involved in the factual, lived situations of Christian men and women whose sexual orientation extends to members of their own sex.

There are weighty reasons for adopting such an approach. For one thing, the relevant theological literature has only very recently begun to incorporate the solid research of the social sciences regarding homosexuality. For another, critical scripture scholarship has called into question many "settled" views about biblical attitudes toward sexuality and homosexuality. These new findings, too, have as yet to be taken into account. Moreover, the positive theology of sexuality is itself in ferment for a variety of reasons, not least of which rise out of recent developments in pharmacology as well as psychology.

More positively, *Another Kind of Love* is primarily an essay in spirituality—an attempt to offer some pastoral suggestions based on six years' experience as a member of a team ministering to gay Catholics and other Christians in the Chicago area. Some first-hand experiences of gay people themselves have been incorporated in order to provide a more concrete account of their situation. These narratives have been altered only to preserve anonymity. I have also asked several gay men and women as well as their relatives and friends to comment on certain subjects, which they have done far more knowledgeably and sensitively than could I have.

By way of personal aside, having written on occultism and the devil, my present effort does not, I assure you, represent a natural thematic progression, except possibly in the sense that all three books resulted from involvement in pastoral situations which most pastors, theologians and spiritual writers happily pass by. A few demons I hope this essay, although devoted to spirituality, will help identify if not exorcize from contemporary society are Hatred, Fear, Willful Misunderstanding, Prejudice and Persecution. If it helps at all, it will have served its purpose.

Writing a book on homosexuality, like perusing one, has its attendant risks. Working with gays has proved somewhat hazardous—doubts, misunderstandings, disagreements, strained relationships, impatience—all have played their possibly necessary role. But the benefits have been far greater. I am beginning to fathom, if only partially and superficially, the oppression and discrimination gay people experience in society and in the church, sometimes throughout a lifetime. I have also come to recognize and appreciate their courage, humanity, and tenacious fidelity to the church as well as their great capacity for laughter, love and sacrifice. Their gratitude for the little the church has done continues to be astonishing.

A certain amount of risk also attends dedicating a book for, on and to "homosexuals." A small book could easily go without. But I wish to take advantage of the opportunity to publish my thanks to those who have shared in this adventure —to Mary Houlihan who began it, to the six priests who have been my teammates these past years, to my Dominican brethren who have so patiently borne with and encouraged me, not least (I think!) to editor Joel Wells who invited me to write the book, and above all to the men and women of Dignity, Chicago, out of whose experience the present book found its meaning and justification.

It is my belief now, as it was my hope six years ago, that the long-overdue ministry to homosexual Christians *as a*

group is a mission of the Holy Spirit in our time, the success
of which will bring the church a major step forward on its
way to catholicism.

Note: In Chicago, early on the Feast of the Assumption,
1977, Mary Houlihan died peacefully in her sleep. A week
later, also in Chicago, shortly before he was to address the International Dignity Convention, Fr. John McNeill was "si-
lenced" for his views on homosexuality by authorities of the
Roman Catholic Church. To both these now silent witnesses
to the Christian dignity of gay men and women, I offer this
edition of *Another Kind of Love* as an inadequate but deeply
felt tribute.

Chapter One
LIVING WITH HOMOSEXUALITY

As dusk fell over the chill city, men and women, singly, in couples and small groups, approach the three-flat and disappear into the late Victorian doorway behind the new brick wall and iron gate. Gathered in the third floor apartment there are soon over forty people—some in their early twenties, a few almost three times that age, the rest around thirty-five or forty. Greeted warmly by the host, most have selected soft or hard drinks to start things off. . . .

Soon, a youthful man steps into the center of the group, most of whom are now seated on borrowed bridge chairs, quietly conversing.

"Let's get started with a prayer, shall we?" The group falls silent.

"Heavenly Father," he continues after a moment, "we have come here tonight to learn about the new rite of reconciliation. . . ."

Lent, 1976. Chicago. Or Boston, Philadelphia, Detroit or Los Angeles. The group, virtually all Catholics, have assembled to watch a filmstrip on the sacrament of penance and share in a discussion to be followed by a short penance service. The speaker who led the opening prayer is a priest. Two other priests are present. I am one of them.

This assembly, which reminded me of accounts of the meetings of early Christians, could have been members of any progressive parish in the country. Except for one circumstance. Most of them were gay.

A few blocks away, thousands of other gay men and women were filling the bars and discotheques that cater to them, where they would dance, drink, meet friends, cruise for "tricks," or just watch the goings-on from the side. On the outskirts of the gay "ghetto," hundreds of men were enjoying the privileges of easy sex in steam baths, whether in elaborate nightclubs or in sleazy hotels. Others cruised the parks and beaches, some were "hustling trade" downtown, still more loitered hopefully in bus and train depots, airports and public lavatories, looking for a contact who was not a police decoy. Still others, usually solitary, probed through murky bookstores for pornographic "cockbooks" or cheap films in arcades, or were sitting in high-priced but uncomfortable seats in roach-infested theaters, watching the endless chain of low-budget, scratchy films depicting genital activities that would strain the imagination of an anatomist.

The vast majority of gay men and women were settling in for an evening of leisure or boredom, both alone and in couples, following the pattern of millions of their straight counterparts in city and suburb from whom they are indistinguishable. Except for one thing. . . .

Somewhere else in the city, a gay teenager, desperate and rejected, would attempt suicide. Another was composing a prize-winning poem. Yet another was shot, trying to rob a liquor store, while some spent the night in silent prayer, their minds seared with love and reaching out in faith to the others in their struggles, sufferings and accomplishments.

Homosexual.

Most of us white, Hibernian, German, Spanish, Slavic and Italian Catholics (or Anglo-Saxon, German or Scandinavian Protestants) grew up with a strong conviction that gay was bad—an attitude characteristic of western civilization, and a feeling not unrelated to our dread of Negroes, Jews, Gypsies or even our half-belief that "the only good Injun is a dead Injun." Good, churchgoing Christians (above all) knew from the Bible that homosexuality was *heinous*. We weren't exactly sure what "heinous" meant, but it was evidently pretty terrible—and excluded someone from the Kingdom of Heaven. Or at least from the church, military service and other respectable associations.

When we were young, "homosexuals" were hardly ever referred to directly, but we knew about taking candy from strangers. . . . For most of us, these attitudes continued through the school years, when we learned jokes we hardly understood about "queers" and "fairies," eventually making the monumental discovery that there were *women* queers, too.

In high school and college, we may have even met "a" homosexual. We probably had suspicions about a few guys, especially the effeminate ones, and maybe even one or two of the tougher girls. But it was usually a fringe phenomenon—hovering uneasily at the far edges of consciousness, except for the jokes and a few novels and perhaps an occasional magazine article or newspaper story. What we never suspected was that the guy in the next room, the basketball star, the spunky red-headed cheerleader who became a nun, the fat kid in architecture who used to laugh so loudly at queer-jokes, the janitor, the dean and the campus cop were all one of "them."

One out of every ten or fifteen persons is homosexual. Gay knows no class differences, religious or ethnic barriers, socioeconomic disparities, sexual or age limits.[1] And if it were illegal to associate with "them," we'd all be in trouble.

For if you are not gay yourself, you *certainly* know someone who is. Among your friends, your co-workers, the doctors who have healed you, the clergy who have ministered to you, your teachers, members of your family, some have been homosexual. Of course, you didn't know it, and probably don't now—in most cases, at least—because they were afraid to tell you. Afraid that you would reject them, perhaps injure them, have them fired or expelled, jailed, publicly disgraced or otherwise victimized.

[1] "Gay" is often used synonymously with "homosexual," but there are significant differences between these terms. "Homosexual" signifies sexual attraction toward members of the same sex, whether or not such attraction is expressed in overt behavior. "Gay" is a wider term, referring primarily to "consciousness"—the awareness and acceptance of homosexual orientation and, to some extent, the sharing of that awareness with others, that is, being "out of the closet." (See p. 62.) Gay consciousness means much more than openly shared homosexual orientation, however. It includes a wide range of personal and social sensibilities differing in significant respects from those of heterosexual ("straight") persons. In this sense, "gay" need not connote sexual activity, though it often does.

For the most part in our culture, gay men and to a lesser extent women have been considered criminal, sick, immoral and predatory misfits worthy of neither pity nor pardon. They have been shunned, hounded, ridiculed, denounced from the pulpit and platform and legislated against. Those convicted of sodomy and other felonious and "unspeakable crimes against God and nature" were often executed, even in recent times, or were given long prison terms. Some men were "mercifully" allowed to submit to castration to avoid decades of imprisonment. Others were forcibly emasculated. Blackmail is still a threat and sometimes an actual occurrence.

I *presume* that these attitudes and practices are more immoral than the acts and persons so severely penalized. However understandable in past ages, such views and atrocities were still inexcusable and are far more so today. Quite simply, I am convinced that the "traditional" civil and religious treatment of homosexuality, based as it largely was on ignorance, fear and fantasy, is now *to that extent* untenable. It is ungodly, inhuman and destructive of individual rights and dignity as well as of the common welfare.

I am further convinced that, as a human condition, homosexuality should not be (as it increasingly *is* not) considered a disease, personal defect, or an emotional disorder. Hence, it is incorrect, misleading and degrading to speak of homosexuality as "curable." It is no less wrong for religious people to label homosexuality a curse, an affliction or a depravity. Nor should all homosexual behavior be condemned in advance as inevitably sinful without much further and more careful study of scripture as well as the many varieties of homosexual experience, attitudes and activities. Similarly, criminal penalties for private sexual acts between consenting adults of any sexual orientation should be abolished; placing such men and women in the same category as rapists, child-molesters, prostitutes and pimps is an injustice no sane society can tolerate, much less the grossly inequitable enforcement of laws frequently practiced by the police and courts, in addition to entrapment, espionage and harassment.

More positively, I also presume (and I hope can show) that homosexual men and women can and do live with freedom and dignity as creative members of society and worthy members of the church. (Although written from a Christian perspective and mainly with Christians in mind, most of what I have to say about the religious situation is, I hope, applicable within the Jewish and Islamic traditions, which share the same biblical heritage.)

The *fact* is that most gay persons are as responsible, dedicated citizens as well as being honest, committed churchgoers as are the rest of the population—a fact borne out by another fact: most homosexual men and women are "invisible"—they cannot be distinguished from the population at large except by their own admission. Yet these same men and women must endure perpetual tension; *they* know that they are "different" in the one respect that, in the somewhat warped mind of western peoples, will overshadow all the others.

Living with homosexuality means, then, living with a difference; doing so well involves developing personal resources and reserves of psychic energy few "straight" people are ever called upon to cultivate or demonstrate. For this reason, one recent study concluded that the "healthy homosexual" is probably *healthier* than the great majority of heterosexual people who, confronted even occasionally by the challenges and conflicts a gay person ordinarily faces daily, would crumble psychologically.[2]

Basically gentle people with a strong aversion to violence and aggression (with, of course, exceptions), *most* gays and lesbians nevertheless possess an internal toughness that enables them to survive the stresses they continually encounter. Sometimes this toughness radiates to the surface of their personalities, and they become hard and bitter—but not often, as far as I can tell. Sometimes the most vulnerable areas of their inner selves are walled off by defensive or evasive attitudes and behavior, but not too frequently. As a result, gay people generally manage to acquire an assortment of psychic scars, but they are rarely disfigured.

Their courageous, flippant, sometimes brazen approach to the "harsh realities" of life reminds me sometimes of the classic circus clown—not the shallow goofiness of Bozo or

[2] Cf. Mark Freedman, "Far from Illness: Homosexuals May Be Healthier Than Straights," *Psychology Today*, Vol. 8, No. 10 (March 1975), pp. 27–33. See below, p. 28.

Ronald McDonald, but the Chaplinesque quality of an
Emmet Kelly, or the great, comic-tragic figures of legend
—Till Eulenspiegel, Scaramouche, Mattachine, Harlequin—
whose attitude affirmed, even in blood, the value of living as
humanly as possible in a world infected by radical evil. Their
secret is courage, love and laughter, an urgent will to savor
the goodness of life in a real and carefree celebration whenever the opportunity can be made to arise.

Perhaps that is why they are called gay . . . even when
being drubbed by the heavies in their blue costumes and
handlebar moustaches. At any rate, there is a clue here worth
considering from a different viewpoint: that of the religious
questioner, who in scouting for meaning in human life, ought
to be alerted by the aura of the mystic and prophet whenever
the clowns come in. Or out. . . .

Later, we shall return to the clowns. Here, to begin with, it
will be necessary to consider briefly the nature of human sexuality in order to grasp something of the meaning and mystery of homosexuality.

THE FOURTEEN SEXES

Biologically, that is, physiologically, the human race can be
divided into male and female adequately, but by no means
perfectly. Sexuality is not defined solely by the presence of
external sex organs or the functions of begetting, conceiving,
and bearing offspring, although the specific attributes of the
two sexes constitute sufficient and necessary criteria to accoun
for fundamentals such as procreation. Considered alone, such
a basis of comparison remains purely physical; it even fails to
take into consideration the associated elements of mating
homemaking and child-rearing practices. Actually, sexuality is
the complex product of at least seven interconnected physio
logical, psychological and sociological systems, rather dif
ferently experienced by males and females, even in the case
of the higher, sub-human mammals. Humanly speaking, there
are also specifically spiritual elements involved—ethics, reli
gious values, aesthetics, and, above all, or underlying all, in
telligence and love.

Biological maleness and femaleness are designations result ing from a complex of five elements: chromosomes, the endocrine glands, hormones, the internal sexual organs and, finally, the external sexual organs. But dynamically, sexual development is a process spanning the temporal spread of a life, beginning with the genetic programming that occurs even before conception and continues through the embryological period, each human person-to-be undergoing many structural changes, including for males the transformation of rudimentary female sex organs into male ones. After birth, the process accompanies further organization of the brain and nervous system, climaxing in much later changes produced by glandular maturation at puberty. Physiological development proceeds along male-female lines through adulthood, menopause and the male climacteric, culminating in senescence.

Individual sexuality is constituted only partially by biological development; also crucially important is the correlative psychosocial process of sexual individuation, from the diffuse experiences of the new-born infant through several intermediate stages leading to eventual maturity. During this process, the two *psychological* elements of sexuality are established: gender *roles* are socially communicated along lines culturally associated with gender *identity*. That is to say, one's sense of masculinity or femininity (role) is not identical with but relative to experienced maleness or femaleness (identity)—the sex "assigned" one at birth and reinforced during rearing.

Sexual "orientation" or "object-choice" seems to be an expression of gender identity, but it is by no means equivalent. In effect, heterosexuality and homosexuality encompass the range of preferences for sexual behavior; they do not constitute gender identity.

A person's gender identity (that is, the awareness of being a male or a female) is generally considered to be at the threshold of fixity by the age of eighteen months; by forty-eight months, identity is normally permanent. Acquiring culturally appropriate gender roles continues for years, however; one learns how to be a boy, or a woman, a father or even a grandmother. It is not simply given in the order of things as if by magic.

Because sexuality is the overall product of a series of complex interactions of various systems, both physical and mental, it has a homeostatic and approximative character. That is, sexuality is a process of many factors *balanced* in a *more or less* specific proportion. Even the ancients knew that nature is only generally constant and predictable: natural elements are *normative,* not exact. Variations *always* surround the nucleus of a general type. Sexual development, too, will be more or less determinate, but greater or lesser normal variations can occur at any point from parental genetic endowment to the last moments of a person's life.

Some effects of physiological and psychological variations will be minor, others will be drastic. Thus, there will be persons who are hermaphroditic—having vestigial organs of the opposite sex, or perhaps who will be sterile, or whose hormonal balance will be different, or whose sex chromosomes will exceed or lack the normal pair. Occasionally, a child is assigned the wrong gender because of small male or large female sex organs and is reared as a member of the opposite sex. Other children are assigned the correct identity, but somehow acquire some of the role characteristics of the opposite sex, resulting in male effeminacy or female masculinity. Sexual orientation is not, however, a function of physiology, gender identification or role characteristics. Sexual preference is learned.

Sexual attitudes and behavior are at least as variable as the respective factors that influence physiological and psychological sexuality. The way in which a child is reared, especially early experiences however remotely connected with sex, will have enormous sexual repercussions in later life. Puberty is an especially critical period of emerging self-definition, but so is menopause, for both men and women in different ways.

Because of the complexities of sexual development, it is not surprising that the social aspect of sexual orientation—who will be a desirable sexual partner—allows for considerable flexibility. The predominant *pattern* will be heterosexual— males and females will be primarily attracted to each other sexually, but hardly to *every* member of the opposite sex. Our preferences are learned responses, like all matters of "taste."

The biological significance of dominant heterosexuality is obvious. But given the apparent "bisexuality" of a large part of the population (as studied by Kinsey and others), that is, the capacity under certain conditions to be attracted to members of either sex, it has become increasingly questionable whether homosexuality or bisexuality fall outside the *normal* range of variation.

Homosexuality seems to be a component factor in most sexual development and behavior in two ways. First, masculinity and femininity as real complementary psychological characteristics are part of everyone's potential character, just as both male and female hormones are present in everyone. Such "bisexuality" enables us to be whole persons, capable of relating to members of both sexes, and comprising necessary qualities of *human* personality. Stifling either of the complementary sexual aspects of our personalities produces fragmentation and often pathological states of mind and behavior, analogous to a deficiency or excess in hormone balance. Developmentally, we incorporate personality traits of *both* our parents (or of other model male and female adults), traits which are not only the basis for being able to relate to members of both sexes, but are themselves part of our fundamental biological constitution. Ordinarily, one aspect of sexual role-potential (and hormones) will predominate, the other recede; both, however, seem very necessary for wholeness.

The second homosexual (or bisexual) personality component is attraction to the same as well as or instead of the opposite sex at some period in life—an attraction that is a *normal* part of the maturation process, but which may never find expression in genital activity. Studies indicate that the majority of males and many females in America and Europe indeed have had some kind of homosexual experience, whether truly genital or not, some time in their lives, usually as a youthful experiment. There is no reason to believe that such isolated experiences are dangerous, evil or sick; presumably, they perform an often important function in the creation of sexual identity. Further, such isolated or passing episodes cannot "reorient" a basically heterosexual person toward exclusive or even predominant homosexuality.

True homosexual persons differ from heterosexual persons mainly in that they prefer members of the same sex as the exclusive or predominant "object" of sexual desire during most of their lives. Most homosexual persons are not exclusively so oriented, however; like the heterosexual population, they can be considered more or less bisexual.

Some homosexuality undoubtedly involves a deep, probably unconscious fear of the opposite sex. It may well stem from a similarly profound sense of sexual inadequacy. But such instances of neurotic development do not apply to all cases of homosexuality, perhaps not even to most. Very many homosexual men and women are in this respect clearly healthy.[3]

From animal studies, it seems evident that in every group of higher mammals at least, there is a wide range of normal sexual behavior, rather than a single type, including at least partial homosexuality.[4] Exclusive homosexuality, however, seems to be a purely human phenomenon. It is certainly true that some homosexual preference and activity has been a human condition from the very start of things and (as far as we know) in every land and culture. Attitudes toward homosexuality or bisexuality, as well as the treatment of homosexual persons, have varied enormously from culture to culture, but the incidence has apparently been statistically rather constant.

To suggest, however, that homosexual preference and activity may be biologically and sociologically within the normal range of behavior is *not* to say that there are no abnormal homosexual conditions, or that homosexual persons do not suffer serious problems. Normality in this regard depends not only upon the persistence of the variation and the margin of variability. In addition, the variation (or "deviation" in sociological jargon) must not be destructive to the individual or to society.

INCIDENCE AND PATHOLOGY

The case for judging the normality of homosexuality (and

[3] Cf. Freedman, art. cit. See also the works listed in the Postlude, pp. 153ff.

[4] Cf. Clellan S. Ford and Frank A. Beach, *Patterns of Sexual Behavior,* New York: Harper & Row, Colophon ed., 1972, pp. 134–43. For a more recent discussion, see Arno Karlen, *Sexuality and Homosexuality A New View,* New York: W. W. Norton and Co., Inc., 1971, pp. 399–434.

other sexual variations) thus depends upon both its status as a statistically constant factor as well as its nonpathological character: is it a sizable and persistent phenomenon, and does it harm individuals or society?

No one knows for sure just how many homosexual persons there are in any actual population, since for the most part, homosexual men and women are indistinguishable from anyone else. In addition, many wish to keep their condition secret. Reliable estimates place the number of *exclusive* homosexuals at about four percent. The number of those who have had some homosexual experience is much higher, about fifty percent. Less than a majority of both men and women have actually experienced significant genital relationships with persons of the same sex, however. It seems reasonable to accept about ten percent as a representative figure for those who are predominantly and exclusively homosexual in orientation and behavior, that is, who have had more than a fleeting homosexual encounter at some time in their lives.[5]

Few students of human sexuality doubt or deny the overall statistical constancy of homosexuality and bisexuality; the real debate concerns the issue of pathology.

Recently, scientific thinking has shifted from a position maintaining that homosexuality is a disease or disorder to one of tolerance or neutrality and in many cases of acceptance as a normal variation. Similarly, in most nations and in seventeen states in America, homosexual relations between consenting adults are no longer considered to be criminal acts. Theologians and church leaders have been much slower in declassifying homosexuality as evil and sinful, but there is a trend in that direction as well.[6]

If a majority of researchers eventually conclude that homo-

[5] These figures reflect the findings of the Institute for Sex Research, Indiana University, as discussed in Wainwright Churchill, *Homosexual Behavior Among Males,* Englewood Cliffs, N.J.: Prentice-Hall, Prism ed., 1971, pp. 50–52.

[6] Cf. Charles Curran, "Homosexuality and Moral Theology: Methodological and Substantive Considerations," *The Thomist,* Vol. 35, No. 3 (July 1971), pp. 447–81. Other theologians include Norman Pittinger, Gregory Baum, Richard McCormick, John Dedek, John McNeill, John Giles Milhaven, references to whose works will be found in the resources listed in the Postlude to this volume.

sexuality is not to be considered in itself a disease, a crime or a sin, but represents a constant, sizable phenomenon in most societies, it would seem reasonable to conclude as well that homosexual preference and some behavior constitute a *normal* and natural part of the order of things. (There are, of course, instances of homosexual attitudes and behavior that are clearly disordered, criminal and evil—just as there are with respect to heterosexuality. The point is that such instances do not typify the majority of persons in either case.)

The shift in scientific, legal and theological thought has by no means completely reversed the former positions, however. Trends notwithstanding, many psychologists still consider homosexuality a disorder, a curable problem akin to alcoholism or various phobias. Several countries (notably Russia and Germany) and thirty-three states in America still penalize homosexuality severely. Many churches anathematize homosexual persons, refuse to license homosexual ministers, and the majority of Christian theologians probably still consider all forms of homosexual activity to be sinful, even if they look on homosexuality itself as merely unfortunate. The debate will certainly continue for some time to come.

Chapter Two
THE MYSTERY OF HOMOSEXUALITY

It is not the purpose of this essay to explore complex questions about the psychological dynamics of sexual development. And fortunately so, for despite the growing amount of information about homosexuality, no one really knows how it comes about. Most "definitive" explanations explain too much or too little; one hypothesis accounts for a few "cases" (usually those it is founded upon), but not for the remaining majority. Cultural differences appear to be more rather than less significant than was previously thought; patterns differ enormously. Published psychological theories directly contradict each other. The experts continue to disagree.

What seems clear is that homosexuality is multi-causal; any number of factors may be involved in each personal history. Consequently, it is a highly variable phenomenon when expressed in behavior. It would be more accurate on the whole to speak of "homosexualities" rather than homosexuality, given the range of differences in origin and expression.

Further, important differences between male and female gay experience are becoming increasingly clear as Lesbians speak out, write more and receive greater attention from researchers. "Gay" hardly covers the full range of male homosexuality, much less that of women. But "Lesbian" itself is similarly inadequate, given the spectrum of attitudes, backgrounds, life-styles and situations gay women experience.[1]

[1] Significantly, there is no corresponding word for "Lesbian" to refer to male homosexuality. Despite some feeling to the contrary among women's groups, I don't think that "gay" should be given that function. Historically, it applied to both sexes and still does in common usage.

It also seems evident that homosexual preference is not strictly innate, that is, a condition rooted in the physiological or psychological make-up of a person, as related above, but is rather a behavioral expression of gender identity acquired at an early age as a disposition which is confirmed by later experience—just as in the case of heterosexual orientation.

But so early does this orientation begin, and so strong is its direction, however unconscious at first, that it *becomes* practically equivalent to an innate personality structure. Such "constitutive" or "constitutional" homosexuality appears to be only minimally subject to later modification, again, just as in the case of constitutional heterosexual preference.

It seems to me that even if the origins (or "causes") of the varieties of homosexual orientation are one day discovered and techniques for altering sexual preference are perfected, homosexuality will still remain a mystery. For, as Marcel might have said, it is not a puzzle to be solved in the laboratory or the psychiatrist's office, but a situation in which men and women are involved and which must be addressed and lived with.

Some gay people have problems, and serious ones, about their sexuality, whether stemming from their own or others' attitudes and behavior, or from a sense of guilt or resentment. Gays also have problems that are distinct from their sexual orientation and its consequences. But most are not problem-ridden neurotics (at least no more so than anyone else!), and to define *them* as a problem because of their sexual preference is the opposite of helping. Over six years of ministering to the gay community has led me to believe that, despite many "common" problems and difficulties, as well as those more typical of homosexual persons, gay men and women are generally ordinary, well-adjusted people who approach life with courage and—importantly—with success. Their stories, and those of their relatives, friends and associates, are an important part of the mystery of human sexuality—much more important, I feel, than the stereotyped but unrepresentative accounts of disturbed gays that cover the pages of so many books written by those whose professional competence lies in treating sickness.

Still, *why* there are homosexual persons remains mysterious. Searching for the meaning and purpose of homosexuality constitutes a profound challenge to many gays, often becoming the dominant context of their relationship with God. One young man wrote to me: "I always hated God for making me a homosexual. After all, he's omnipotent and could do all or everything. Therefore, he could have made me straight. But I've lately felt there must have been a reason, but God only knows why."

As we shall see later on, the religious moment of faith for many gay men and women often comes as a meaning-giving experience of acceptance from a source beyond themselves. Others, hurt and confused by the mystery of their situation as well as by rejection, turn to God in their need: "At the start I didn't really feel any change. To me being gay and Catholic were completely compatible. But in high school, as more and more of my friends became interested in girls and I had no such feelings, I turned to God more often as my concern increased. You might say that I used Him as a shoulder to cry on."

The Christian response to the mystery of homosexuality does lie, I think, in attempting to see the situation of gay men and women in the context of God's purposes—although what those plans are, we may never know. And although both individual and social destiny must remain to some extent enshrouded in mystery and thus an occasion for faith and hope, I think it is possible to discern something of the meaning of homosexuality in a religious sense—not completely, but more as a hint or a suggestion. That, however, must wait for a later chapter.

LESBIANISM

Lesbian experience is possibly even more highly variegated than male gay experience. Many women, perhaps the majority of Lesbians, mature lacking any sexual interest in men and gravitate naturally to gay relationships. Others identify themselves as Lesbian for reasons far different from sexual orientation alone. As with a surprisingly large number of gay men, many come out after years of heterosexual marriage, often being mothers of children. Having been patronized, restricted, emotionally and perhaps even physically abused by their husbands, these women seek the company of those who can most easily understand and support them, either for a time or permanently. In some cases, such women are not looking for sex at all and in fact can be called homosexual only in a limited sense.

As noted elsewhere in this book, pseudohomosexuality, a term coined by Dr. Lionel Ovesey, has been used almost exclusively to refer to men who resort to homosexual behavior in order to cope with unconscious needs for power or dependency.[2] Similarly, many women who adopt a homosexual life-style because of problems or difficulties, perhaps irreversible ones, are not truly homosexual, for physical experience is not the real goal of their relationships. They can be called Lesbian or gay, however, because of the emotional fulfillment they seek and often find in same-sex relationships. Such relationships need not be considered compensation in a pathological sense, for they may well represent a positive adjustment, that is, one which significantly reduces anxiety.

Further, many heterosexual women who have experienced difficulty in married life seek out the companionship of gay men to find the kind of non-threatening masculinity they desire, either provisionally or indefinitely.[3] While these women should not be called Lesbian, they could probably be considered gay since they associate with gay men and inhabit a niche in the gay world. (Calling them "fag-hags" or "fruit flies" is objectionable, despite the emotional predation some may manifest. For openly ridiculing such women while allowing them freely to associate in gay men's haunts is merely another incursion of the macho mystique into the gay world. Tagging someone a "fag-hag" implicitly degrades gay men themselves as it demeans the women they so label.)

Thus, like their male counterparts, Lesbians may fear, hate, tolerate or like and even love members of the opposite sex—both gay and straight. But they prefer their own sex. Being

[2] Lionel Ovesey, *Homosexuality and Pseudohomosexuality*, New York: Science House, 1969.

[3] A sympathetic portrayal of one such woman can be found in Wallace Hamilton's romantic novel *Coming Out*, New York: Signet, 1977.

aware of and accepting themselves as gay is what Lesbian means. It is much more than sexual orientation or even being "out." Nor is Lesbianism "a matter of gender-role designation, but contains within it elements of psychological, emotional and spiritual involvement."[4] Part of the spiritual involvement in Lesbianism is a social consciousness, a sense of belonging to a vast sisterhood whose immediate destiny is closely linked with women's liberation throughout the world. In many respects, Lesbianism can be described more accurately as an emotional and spiritual solidarity in which sexual behavior has a real but more subsidiary value than it does for male gays, for whom emotional companionship and political solidarity are generally of less immediate importance.

Among male gays, too, however, sexual gratification alone is probably overrated as the prime factor in relationships—both long- and short-term. That is, there may well be deeper motives involved in forming a gay relationship, including symbolic values. While many lovers have told me that were it it not for the physical relationship, they would not likely even be friends, I know of many gay couples who remain faithfully together but who have no common sex life—or very little—because of age, accident or other physical or psychological dispositions.

Operative in the difference between male and Lesbian experience here is, I think, more the fundamental psycho-physiological and sociological differences between the sexes than the more particular differences between Lesbians and male gays. Importantly, gays of both sexes have proved themselves capable of transcending these differences by means of motives other than psycho-physical attraction alone. I am referring here to the specifically human and therefore spiritual values of care, fidelity, trust and commitment. But the fundamental differences between male and female sexuality make it more difficult for gays than for straights to appreciate each other's values and life-styles.

Thus the "nesting" or domestic proclivities of Lesbians, in contrast to the more restless and public behavior of male gays, owe something to their fundamental femaleness, just as

---

[4] Martin and Lyon, op. cit., p. 19.

the excursions of gay men have a real psycho-physiological basis. Strict segregation of the sexes in the gay world extenuates these fundamental traits to the point of caricature. There is cause, therefore, to welcome greater contact among Lesbians and male gays, and some evidence that such affectionate association is increasing, along with greater mutual understanding and appreciation. A bar such as His and Hers in Chicago provides a case in point.

LIVING GAILY

Human sexuality, as should be obvious by now, is complex, variable and processive, that is, developmental. Heterosexuality, while the dominant direction of genital interest in human persons, is not sharply defined, but exists as a disposition more or less conjoined with the capacity for and perhaps the expression of homosexual interest in all but a small fraction of the male and female population.

Suppressing one's homosexual capacities is destructive of integral personhood just as is suppressing one's heterosexual capacities. As the foundation for friendships between members of the same sex, these capacities must be cultivated and carefully integrated into the overall pattern of life experiences. This is *not* to say that genital homosexual or heterosexual activities should be casually or deliberately engineered "in order to find out what it's all about." Sexual experimentation, while perhaps tolerable in adolescent behavior, is immature and depersonalizing for adults, just as much as promiscuity is.

In fact, the great majority of men and women are simply not "turned on" for the most part by the prospect of genital intimacy with someone of the same sex—or, in the case of homosexual persons, the opposite sex. Nevertheless, "bisexuality" as the human capacity for love and affection for both men and women is a necessary component of full human development. (It is important to bear in mind that if, at some moment in a person's life, this "bisexual" capacity is expressed in terms of genital experience, that does not constitute the person "a" bisexual any more than an isolated homosexual or heterosexual encounter makes someone "a" homosexual or heterosexual.)[5]

The suppression of bisexual capacities occurs by either avoiding the company of men or women, usually because of sexual fears, or by stifling any realization of affection for those unavoidably encountered in the course of business, recreation, worship, etc. Bereft of the human dimension of affectivity, such relationships, although common to both gay and straight people, are harmful to individual growth and social well-being. Human associations are turned into mechanical affairs of utility or convenience, possibly of mutual, but superficial, enjoyment. Real affection, lasting concern and intimacy are precluded from the outset. The loss of potential richness and creativity in such experiences is incalculable.

Gay advocates and psychologists have coined the term "homophobia" to refer to the unhealthy state of fear, aversion and hatred many, perhaps most, straight persons feel when they encounter or even think about homosexuality, whether in themselves or others. There is a complementary attitude that is just as crippling and objectionable among gays, however; it might as well be called "heterophobia"—the unreasonable fear of the opposite sex, usually associated, as in the case of homophobia, with repulsive fantasies of genitals or sexual intercourse. Both of these irrational attitudes may be converted into expressions that are sexist and demeaning, whether directed at all gays (or straights), or at males or females of either sexual orientation. Thus arises, for instance, the more or less voluntary segregation of gay men and lesbians within gay institutions and activities. The sad and debilitating moral diseases traditionally given long Greek names, misogyny and misanthropy, know no barriers of race, creed, color *or* sexual preference.

Several positive attitudes can be singled out as particularly

[5] The words "homosexual," "heterosexual," "bisexual" and "sexual" are, properly speaking, adjectives, not nouns, referring to one aspect of personality—sexual orientation. To use them as nouns reflects a common but wrong-headed propensity to equate personality with sexuality. Despite the existence of a homosexual subculture, a person is not "a" homosexual in anything like the sense of being "a" woman, "a" Republican or "an" Australian.

important with regard to living creatively as or with a gay person, and I wish here to devote some discussion to them.

ACCEPTANCE

Living with homosexuality involves, first of all, acceptance: accepting yourself, if you are gay—or accepting your gay friend, relative or associate. Acceptance here does not mean mere resignation to the inescapable—"nothing more can be done," nor does it mean "bearing one's cross," a burden, trial or temptation, much less a punishment for God knows what infraction of the celestial rules. Rather, acceptance means an affirmation of yourself or another "as is," a decision which demands an end to resentment, self-dissection, worry and doubt. Acceptance means saying yes to what we all genuinely are, faults and all, but not to the myths, stereotypes and fantasies which distort our perceptions and rule our expectations of what we and others should be.

Affirming your own worth—or another's—in the midst of a world that continually declares your worthlessness as vile, dangerous and sick, is hardly easy. But it can be done—by refusing to acquiesce in the world's verdict, and by resolutely cultivating the positive talents, qualities, skills and capacities you are gifted with in whatever degree.

The greatest enemy of self-acceptance is probably a sense of guilt merely for being what you are. Such guilt, however, is rarely a personal reaction to wrong freely done, but the internalization of society's disparagement: an impersonal and unjust rejection communicated by a thousand gross and subtle means.

Acquital does not usually come by a change in social norms, but by the realization that such norms are not only relative, but frequently wrong. Liberation from social guilt results from deliberate disengagement from society's totalitarian claims, not in the form of complete anarchy, but more as a mode of detachment in the religious sense. The independence many gays achieve by choosing to live by their own freely chosen values not only provides them with a measure of social autonomy that makes for psychological health, but it also contributes *to* society, for gays thus acquire a keen critical

sense. They have learned about the emperor's new clothes
. . . and don't hesitate to say so.

Many gays' deep sense of personal guilt often has a religious quality about it, a feeling of damnation. Again, this is
often "merely" the inner version of what parents and churchmen preach at them, a condemnation reiterated in many ways
in daily life. Again, too, such judgments are impersonal and
arbitrary, netting all and sundry in the generalizations of self-
righteousness. But *God* does not curse anyone "from his
mother's womb."

I shall have more to say later on about the place of religion
in gay life; here, I wish only to note that by accepting homosexuality as a component of their personalities, gays can also
accept it "graciously" as part of the divine design for human
existence. By so doing, they can make their sexuality—their
humanly ordinary but vast capacity to give and receive love—
into an occasion for personal growth and sanctity, that is,
wholeness. Only by denying and rejecting so intimate a portion of their personality can their homosexuality become for
gays a curse, an obstacle to happiness and an excuse for
failing to make the most of life. Bitterness, resentment and
misery must follow, or—at best—the needless excision of part
of themselves as the terrible price exacted for entry into the
Kingdom of Heaven. Such an act of self-destruction is not
only unnecessary, but evil; it produces not saints but psychological cripples.

Parents, friends and associates such as teachers and pastors, should no more blame themselves for the homosexuality
of someone they care for and may have been responsible for,
than they should blame him or her. It is not a question of
blame, failure or retribution, not even of cure, but rather of
accepting a fact about a person who deserves and probably
desperately needs love and support at a critical moment in
life. Accepting a gay person does not mean approving everything gay; it merely means recognizing that he or she is a valuable, lovable and vulnerable person for whom life will have
sufficient pain without the added burden of rejection.

When young persons, in trust and hope, reach out and
confide in someone they esteem that they are gay, a response
of grief, anger or denial can effect almost irreparable harm.

The young, however, have no monopoly on sensitivity and vulnerability; it can take far greater courage for adults to reveal themselves to a cherished friend, parent, or, indeed, a spouse or children, for the risk of rejection can be far more threatening. Humiliation can be complete and final; public exposure can bring lasting ruin.

Self-acceptance must eventually find its ground and validation in acceptance by others; the radical self-acceptance which constitutes an act of faith in life's meaning and value even when rejected by friends, family and acquaintances can only rise from a more fundamental Source, whose acceptance is absolute and unconditional. As we have already seen, for some gays faith in God often coincides with self-acceptance in just this way—being accepted not *despite* what they are, but *for* what they are and what they can become. The deep reassurance that they are loved in turn enables them to share that acceptance with others. One young woman of twenty-nine put it thus: "My feelings toward God have something to do with how I feel that He feels about me; and, consequently, how I feel about myself. As my self-esteem increases, I find that I am better able to be responsive to God and to others."

Acceptance, then, rests upon compassion as well as affirmation. It finds expression in thanksgiving and celebration. As someone expressed it: "My homosexuality has not in any way affected my appreciation, devotion, or love for God. Since the age of 12, when I first realized my sex-role, I have continually thanked God for making me what I am—first and foremost, one of His creatures . . . providentially made to live as I am in this age of history, and secondarily, a gay person. I had no choice in being born gay or hetero; rather, I was given my human nature and 'beingness' from the Being of all beings! I sincerely feel that we have to accept what and who we are, and accept it with our hearts . . . never feeling different from others, but rather as being part of Divine Providence, the Divine Plan!"

The evident presence of self-affirmation, compassion and thankful celebration in the gay community, even though frequently disguised, indicates to me not only the basic health there, but also the radical religious character latent in gay experience.

Living creatively with homosexuality does not end with acceptance, but begins with it. At least two further elements are essential: association and action.

SOLIDARITY

Real and continuous contact with *both* gay and straight people is necessary for effective living in a world that is neither wholly straight nor gay. Isolation means loneliness and one or another form of estrangement, which is a way of saying incomplete development as a human person. The "healthy homosexual" man or woman can be shown to have a gay support group as well as heterosexual friends and acquaintances. The loner as well as the "heterophobe" is usually headed for problems.

Association finds expression in solidarity and friendship. Both are important, but it is friendship that is indispensable. Intimacy among friends is not restricted to genital experience; in fact, for many gays, "having sex" may be the least likely event in which they experience true closeness. Without intimacy, life is reduced to the mechanical relationships we call games or simply deprived of all human warmth.

SERVICE

Action is probably the natural outgrowth of solidarity and compassion; it is impossible for many not to do something to improve the lot of their struggling brothers and sisters once they have experienced the real liberation of acceptance and radical affirmation. For some, the form action will take is political. For others, service of various kinds.

Both gays and straights will have to work together rather than merely protest injustices in order to reform a prejudicial legal system and to bring about new legislation guaranteeing equal rights and opportunity in housing, employment and other areas of civil life. Serious and sincere dialogue with church leaders and theologians must likewise replace merely polemical confrontations.

Gays must also recognize that much of their difficulties and suffering result from the destructive agencies within gay culture itself. The struggle for liberation entails the correction of these elements, too—whether the defensive psychic and social structures erected by any beleaguered minority, or the deliberate exploitation of gays by other gays themselves. Gays, too, are the perpetuators as well as the victims of their own sexual myths and manipulative behavior. Here again, only the truth of lives well-lived can convince and liberate.

In religious language, the "vocation" of gays is thus not only to accept themselves as God accepts them, and to work to bring about an end to repression and injustice, but also to redeem the gay world itself.

REDEEMING THE GAY WORLD

Gay Christians need not forsake the gay world any more than any Christian need forsake the world in order to be saved. But like the Christian-in-general, the gay Christian, while in the world is not *of* it—that is, not its creature. Like other Christians, gay men and women must be *for* the world, including the gay world in so far as it is not wholly inimical to their own welfare or irreconcilably opposed to Christian values. The Christian is called (and sent) to any place where redemption is warranted.

The gay world is permeated with positive values, many of them, however, less evident than its defects and dangers—none of which I intend to minimize. But to overlook the generosity, compassion, community-feeling, and real love present there would be an even greater disservice. Real human (and therefore Christian) values exist in the gay world, and it is thus redeemable and, indeed, in some measure redeemed and redemptive.

Again, like the larger world of which it is a token, the gay world is a dangerous place, physically as well as morally. But *as* a microcosm, the gay world richly illustrates both the opportunity and the means by which the Christian reconstruction of the world can proceed, especially in terms of the whole realm of sexuality.

Life in the so-called straight world can also be endlessly bitter, or it can be the occasion for enjoyment and achievement for gay men and women not so much *as* gay, but primarily as persons who also happen to be gay. The cost of success, however, is perseverance, faithfulness and integrity—qualities by no means lacking among gays. The penalty for withdrawal, capitulation and evasion will be not only a stunted social life, but the perpetuation of oppression from without and exploitation from within the gay community. On the other hand, a flippant militancy can also fan dwindling embers of prejudice into new flames of persecution. What is called for in the realm of action is judgment and skill as well as courage and resilience.

For the most part, the "secret" (if any) of living with homosexuality—especially for those "ungifted" gays who are not blessed with outstanding talents, skills or even courage—is a relatively simple thing: living with compassion and honesty, with oneself and others, both gay and straight. While no different in their need for love and justice, dignity and meaning, gays often face obstacles no straight person is ever likely to encounter in the pursuit of happiness. Consequently, their ways of overcoming these obstacles will be to some extent distinctive. But straight people should have no great difficulty with that; the values and beliefs are common. Despite that fundamental sameness, for gays the "courage to be" —the willingness to make life rich in meaning and devotion —also requires the strength to be different and the nerve to celebrate that difference as a gift and an opportunity.

Chapter Three
LIVING IN A STRAIGHT WORLD

What we now call "Western Civilization" has been characterized for several thousand years by an uncomfortable interest in sex which amounts to a virtual preoccupation. In sexual matters, as in law, politics, philosophy, medicine, science, education and religion, the forebears of what we claim as our Judeo-Christian tradition were mainly the Greeks, the Jews, the Romano-Italic peoples and the Germanic tribes of northwestern Europe. The Greeks and Romans contributed a certain enthusiasm for the varieties of sexual experience, while from the Germans and Jews we derived an often conflicting demand for control and restriction.

Our religious and ethical attitudes toward sexuality are particularly indebted to the severe, almost puritanical code of the patriarchal Jews which distinguished their worship and morality from those of surrounding peoples, especially, in the three pre-Christian centuries of Hellenic cultural influence and Alexandrian conquest, that of the Greeks.

While never totally successful, even in ancient times, this more or less monolithic sexual code has been eroded, if not cracked, within the last century by the pressure of the social sciences and psychiatry, coupled with the fracture of the supportive substrata of authoritarian philosophy and theology. But despite a shift in our attitudes (the so-called "sexual revolution"), actual deviation, especially homosexuality, has by no means become tolerable to modern society. Gays still live in an officially straight and therefore largely unsympathetic world, however unlikely actual persecution may be.

In this and the following chapter, I intend to explore a few

possibilities with regard to sexual co-existence, presuming that
the number of gay persons in our society will remain constant, as will the general disapproval of most other people. It
may help to reduce mutual antagonism by examining some of
the prevalent myths about homosexuality, both those of the
straight and the gay world. In the interest of non-gay readers,
I shall also conduct a short "tour" of the gay world. But my
central concern will be to inquire how gays can traverse the
border between the gay and straight world without personal
diminishment, a feat which will become more and more de-
pendent upon a mutual willingness of gays and straights to
co-exist, to evaluate attitudes and ideas, and, if necessary, to
alter them.

A LEGACY OF OPPRESSION

Homosexual behavior among men, and occasionally among
women, has been strongly condemned in the civil and especially the religious laws of most western peoples throughout
history. Even in Greece, homosexuality was generally considered to be a perversion, contrary to popular belief. Solon
decreed death as the penalty in Athens for the attempted se-
duction of youths. It is questionable whether the sentence was
ever carried out, however. The Torah also prescribed death as
the punishment for homosexual acts (Lev. 20:13)—probably by stoning. Again, there are no accounts of actual executions in the Bible, unlike instances of heterosexual punishment for crimes such as adultery and rape. (The destruction
of Sodom and Gomorrah was probably not merely because of
"sodomy," even if such a thing were actually attempted by
the otherwise truly unpleasant Sodomites.)

The New Testament also records no actual punishments for
homosexual behavior, nor do any early Christian documents,
despite several general condemnations. The first mention of
the death penalty occurred in an imperial decree from the
year 342 AD. An edict of Theodosius in 390 specified burning at the stake for both homosexual offenses and heresy.
Burning would remain the "usual" legal penalty for over a
thousand years to come, but few if any actual instances of ex-
ecution can be cited before the fifteenth century.

It was not until the time of the Spanish Inquisition that homosexual acts were punished to any large extent by death, but even then leniency was the general rule in practice. Perhaps fifty to one hundred persons were executed in all. During the era of the Reformation and the wars of religion and up to the nineteenth century, possibly two hundred more victims went to the stake or gallows, or were beheaded, drowned, strangled, or even buried alive.

Compared to the *millions* of Moslems, Jews, Greek Orthodox, Albigensians, Protestants, Catholics, "witches" and even real criminals officially murdered between the tenth and twentieth centuries, comparatively few homosexual men and women were killed. But actual executions should not be taken as the sole index of oppression; confiscation, imprisonment, exile, torture, mutilation, fines and public humiliation were likewise employed—when, as with capital punishment, it so suited the state or church. Perhaps the most destructive form of oppression was (and is) the constant weight of civil and ecclesiastical reprobation loaded on homosexual persons, whether publicly or in the solitude of their own minds.

The single most horrible instance of gay persecution occurred, not surprisingly, during Hitler's Third Reich. Known homosexual persons in Germany and occupied countries were rounded up and sent to concentration camps. Forced to wear pink triangles to proclaim their crime—similar to the Jews' yellow Star of David—over 220,000 gays were slaughtered by the Nazis, according to reliable sources. Those who survived the holocaust were not allowed, as criminals, to receive compensation when "liberated" by the Allies.[1]

Today, as in past ages, cruel and unusual punishment is still meted out to gays, often in the form of lengthy prison sentences. But official acts of condemnation do not comprise the major harassment, oppression and daily stress that gays must endure or succumb to. Although no longer executed, they are often abused by police, the press and politicians. Homosexual "witch hunts," instigated even in recent decades to ruin or threaten political figures or to bolster the image of their rivals, have generally destroyed only the little fry who lacked sufficient power, money or prestige to avoid being netted.

[1] Cf. Louis Crompton, "Gay Genocide: From Leviticus to Hitler," Module #10, Salvatorian Justice and Peace Commission, Milwaukee: no date, p. 8.

More subtly, known homosexual persons are often denied equal protection; the selective enforcement of laws equally applicable to heterosexual and homosexual "crimes" often singles out gays for punishment and public disgrace. The armed forces "separate" admitted gays from service with a "less than honorable" discharge, if not dishonorably after a court martial. Employees of all kinds, but especially teachers and government officials have been summarily fired even on the mere suspicion of being homosexual. Others are forced to resign. Many seminaries and religious orders refuse to accept candidates who are or who appear to be homosexual; suspected homosexuality is likewise sufficient warrant for expulsion. Gay ministers are likely to be deprived of their calls. For some victims of such thorough social oppression, society's final act of vengeance is the coroner's verdict of suicide, and not infrequently of murder.

The murder of Robert Hillsborough in San Francisco in June 1977 tragically illustrates how anti-gay sentiment expressed in a publicly irresponsible manner can contribute to violence and crime. In the midst of the anti-gay rights campaign centered on the Dade County, Florida, referendum, Hillsborough was singled out for an unprovoked and brutal attack by four youths. His killers stabbed Hillsborough fifteen times with a hunting knife. Two of the assailants were convicted, one of second-degree murder, the other of aggravated assault. Another was granted immunity for testifying against his companions, while the fourth was tried in juvenile court. In connection with the murder, a $5 million lawsuit was filed against Anita Bryant and her Save Our Children crusade by Hillsborough's mother and his lover. While unsuccessful, the suit points out how pressure against gays generated by self-righteous citizens publicly concerned about law and order can become, ironically, an incentive to crime. For it easily justifies violent abuse of those already targeted for hostility and persecution. Even sadder is the fact that such has been the perennial lot of minority groups throughout the long history of "civilization."[2]

[2] For similar accounts, see also David Kopay and Perry Young, op. cit., pp. 219–20, and John McNeill, *The Church and the Homosexual*, Kansas City: Sheed, Andrews and McMeil, Inc., 1976, p. 158.

GAY RESISTANCE AND LIBERATION

Beginning with the "Stonewall Riot" following a raid on a New York gay bar in 1969, when the customers unexpectedly resisted arrest, the "gay rights" movement in America has been offering increased resistance to both overt and clandestine oppression, often aided by civil liberties groups. Legal action against the military, city, state and federal governments, industries, social organizations and even religious bodies has brought about some changes, as have protests, demonstrations, petitions and campaigns. The emergence of a "gay press" has added to the growing power of resistance.

Often the specific aims of such efforts are not well-defined; sometimes they are acutely focused. But overall, they seem to be bringing about a mood of increased tolerance if not acceptance. Even celebrations such as Gay Pride week, the annual commemoration of the Stonewall Riot, with its speeches, workshops, parties and parade, have accomplished much in the way of softening public attitudes.

Some involvement in or at least support of political efforts to end discrimination is probably not only necessary at this time for gays in order to sustain the impetus of the movement toward greater acceptance, but also health-producing as a manifestation of solidarity with other gays and as a participation in social process. By such action and support, gays appropriate their own political destiny—a requirement for responsible citizenship in a free society. But efforts to bring the straight world to its knees, to exact "reparations" for past injustices, or to achieve massive political concessions are both unrealistic and counterproductive—not merely because they will not work, but because they concentrate on the sins of the past rather than on present needs and future possibilities.

As further gains are made, and gays are allowed to assume their rightful place in society as responsible citizens, able leadership in the gay community will become even more important. Those who now merely, if artfully, verbalize gays' complaints against the straight world are not likely to be as able to sponsor positive contributions to a saner, more humane world embracing both gays and straights. Further, it

will take immense discernment and skill to guide constructive
collaboration with the straight world without sacrificing the
valuable countercultural elements in the gay world—elements
laden with corrective, prophetic potential.

CULTURAL OPPRESSION AND
EMANCIPATION

Political oppression and resistance are not the only dialec-
tical factors involved in the struggle toward true sexual emancipation. Cultural oppression of gays has been no less prevalent, and possibly more damaging to their human dignity
cultural resistance is no less needed.

Gays have been ridiculed and lampooned since the come-
dies of Aristophanes and the satires of Lucan and Horace
more often than not, viciously. In our own time, despite occasional attempts at sympathetic, even honest treatment, novels
and films have generally portrayed gays in stereotypical poses
Gay men are more often than not effeminate "fags," fey and
not only unhappy, but dead by the last chapter or reel. The
same is true of lesbians, who tend to appear "butch" and cal-
lous as well as not a little sick. Few homosexual roles in film
or on stage have ever presented a truly human, healthy and
even remotely well-adjusted gay person—despite the fact tha
several well-known screen and stage writers are themselves
homosexual. The paying public still gets what it wants.

As a mirror of their situation, films, plays and most novels
have reflected a distorted image of gays' lives, reinforcing
popular myths and perpetuating stereotypes. Gay films, magazines and novels, mainly a species of soft to hard-core pornography, are no less oppressive and distorted, in so far as
they feature counter-myths and stereotypes, fantasy and sex
ual escapism of the most adolescent stripe. While possibly
more understandable, the market-determined themes and
treatment in gay literature and films are no more excusable
than those dredged up by the straight establishment. Both are
detrimental to forming healthy attitudes, values and patterns
of behavior, pandering to the lowest levels of prurience and
escapism, rather than offering plausible models for authentic
admiration and imitation.

Rather than burying themselves in the vast sands of the television wasteland in search of alternative entertainment, gays should participate fully in the best cultural life accessible in society, exercising critical judgment and expressing their views about the presentation of gay as well as other themes. For instance, the gay Media-watch, established to detect prejudicial treatment (mainly on television), far from being a form of censorship, is itself a responsible exercise of freedom of expression. Individuals, too, should not only demand fair representation in the media, but should express their appreciation for honest attempts to explore the gay situation. Sensationalism should be particularly attacked as a distortion and as a vehicle for commercial exploitation.

Gay artists involved in the media and the theater should similarly strive to correct the distorted image of gays not only in major films, but perhaps especially in gay-produced films. Rather than crusading against the pornographic image, usually a futile endeavor, gays should work toward creating a humane alternative.

Several recent films provide outstanding examples of film art and gay consciousness: the Canadian feature *Outrageous,* and especially the privately produced, superb gay documentaries *Word Is Out* and *Gay USA.* Some commercial films such as *Sunday Bloody Sunday, Boys in the Band* and *A Taste of Honey* now rank as classics, while *Staircase, The Ritz* and *Norman, Is That You?* are better off forgotten along with the murky adaptation of Tennessee Williams' *Suddenly Last Summer.* Most good gay films have been based on even better plays, such as *Fortune and Men's Eyes.* As gay themes in cinema mature, the gay theater is showing signs of even further progress, to mention only *Streamers* and *Crimes Against Nature.*

TACIT OPPRESSION

Oppression need not be overt, nor even consciously in the mind of victim or oppressor to be effective; jokes and pointed remarks have always been used to put down despised groups of all kinds: "Can anything good come out of Nazareth?" The most insidious and destructive examples of society's negation of gays are probably covert forms of indoctrination. The emergence of the feminist liberation movement has illuminated this shadowy side of social conditioning with regard to childhood experiences, which are even more problematic for gays and lesbians than for straight women.

Children's play is not merely fun and games; in every culture, childhood is also a rehearsal period for acquiring skills and learning roles for later social existence. Typically (or, more accurately, stereotypically), little girls are given "baby" dolls that now urinate and vomit and are encouraged to play house; they are presented with tea-sets and tiny ovens, frilly aprons and cardboard or plastic "people" dolls with extensive wardrobes. They are discouraged from roughhousing, climbing trees, playing with marbles, tops, yo-yo's, toy guns, knives or swords and other unladylike occupations. Boys, of course, are encouraged to do everything girls are not supposed to; they are given footballs, toy animals, hammers and saws, trucks and fire engines, as well as a variety of guns, planes, tanks and other war toys but are not allowed to play with dolls past a very tender age, nor do any of the "silly" things girls do, such as learn how to cook, sew, shop, clean house or tend babies.

While it would be absurd, and in fact impossible, to abolish the childrearing practices of our culture, it should be realized that the attitudes conveyed by such conditioning embody highly questionable assumptions about masculine and feminine roles, behavior and status in society, many of which should be changed. Some child psychologists are campaigning for such changes.

Certain attitudes are particularly inimical to full human development and need radical improvement—the myth, for instance, that men (and, ergo, little boys) are tough and probably dirty, logical, unemotional, competitive and better than women (and, ergo, little girls) and must therefore dominate them. Women are, in contrast, weak, soft, emotionally fragile, needful of protection, guidance and a strong male presence to serve and obey.

Residual nineteenth-century fantasies like the myth of the nuclear family, gender roles such as those just caricatured nevertheless still exist, powerfully underpinning much of the oppressive sexual conditioning in our society. They are neither Christian nor even healthy. Translated into adult behavior, they emerge as operational beliefs such as that of male supremacy or *machismo*—the notion that women exist to satisfy the male's sexual needs which, being irrepressible, if not insatiable, must inevitably find genital expression, given even the slightest opportunity. A good deal of male adolescent energy is supposedly devoted to creating such opportunities, or, in the case of girls, avoiding them. The actual situation is more likely one of a mutual fear of inadequacy coupled with a sense of pressure to perform, often bolstered by noisy bravado and accounts of various exploits—a combination of factors which, converted into behavioral values, has ruined countless marriages and created crucifying feelings of inferiority among both gay and straight men and women.

"Pseudo-homosexuality" is, in many cases, a way out of the sexual rat-race for straight men who cannot or will not conform to the expectations of the *macho* male stereotype. The "feminine" values of true homosexual males, especially those who are not effeminate, severely challenge the *macho* mystique. The usual response is violent repudiation, whether verbal or physical.

Lesbians are even more threatening to images of male superiority for, in effect, the message they embody is that men are sexually superfluous, if not an annoyance. The *macho* rejoinder has been to elevate photographic lesbianism to the level of sexual fantasy in "men's" magazines, reinforcing the myth that all women are merely sexual toys. But the dominant male image also forbids admitting, much less expressing, any deep affection for other men as well as women, if for no other reason than the deep fear of being thought "queer."

One of the great contributions the mere presence of gay men and women provides a society dominated by truly demonic sexual images and ideologies is the concrete critique of such myths and stereotypes. Homosexuality is a countercultural corrective, and in that sense, prophetic.

GAY MYTHS AND STEREOTYPES

The distorted thinking, projections and unreal images that plague the whole realm of sexuality trouble male-female rela-

tionships seriously; they also create particularly difficult situations for gays. By "myths," I am here referring to fanciful
and prejudicial misconceptions about gays' sexual identity,
role and behavior, which are shared by a large segment of the
population, including some gays themselves. Similarly, "stereotypes" are images uncritically thought to be representative of
all gay persons and hence of each. Myths, based on stereotypical thinking, determine various attitudes and behavior,
most of which are unfortunate in their consequences, and not
for gays alone.

The most obvious and pervasive stereotypes identify gays
in terms of inverted gender roles: male gays are thought to be
effeminate, arch and willowy "fairies" and "faggots," while
lesbians are rough, mannish, close-cropped "dykes." Various
corollaries follow: the (erroneous) belief that gays can be
recognized by clothing, body type, a certain "veiled" look in
their eyes, the way they strike matches or examine their
fingernails. The stereotyped "fruit" is a hairdresser, interior
decorator, ballet dancer or actor—the "lesbo" is a truck-
driver, wrestler or telephone installer. Sexual behavior is
imagined to follow lines of inverted heterosexual roles
(themselves largely mythical): an active, aggressive "male"
and a passive, receptive "female." A further corollary is the
belief that all gays are sex-obsessed, their whole existence
centered on bed.

Most myths and stereotypes have a core of fact; the truth
here is that some, if very few, gays *are* effeminate or
mannish, etc. But the major fact is that the great majority of
gay men and lesbians are just like everyone else, except for
their sexual preferences, and in that different not so much in
kind as in degree. When thinking of a "typical" gay person,
then, we might as well include Wyatt Earp and Emily Dickin-
son alongside Oscar Wilde and Gertrude Stein. It nevertheless
seems to be the case that gays as a whole are more gentle and
have greater sensitivity than equally representative straights;
that is, on matched personality tests, gays frequently (not always) score lower on aggression—Billy the Kid notwithstanding—and higher on aesthetic awareness, the appreciation
of beauty. Hence, many gays may "naturally" gravitate to the
arts. But many also gravitate to the military. . . .

Less is known about lesbians than gay men (perhaps because almost all sex researchers have been male). But at least with regard to male homosexuality, a man comfortable with his sexual orientation, however large or small an element in his self-awareness, is more open than the *macho* male (and no doubt his female equivalent) to realms of human experience foreclosed to the latter by the necessity of preserving the image of "he-man" toughness—an image lampooned as much by the "rhinestone cowboy" stars of country music fame as it is by the motorcycle club members who favor "leather and chains" gay bars.

Among the most prevalent myths concerning homosexuality, again sometimes shared by gays, are the beliefs that homosexual orientation is somehow chosen; that it is (conversely) a disease that "spreads," can be caught by the unwary or unprotected, and increases with toleration; that it is a permanent, static condition; that it is caused by something or someone; that gays are promiscuous and that, as a result, gay relationships are unstable and short-lived; and, most destructive of all, that gays are immoral child-molesters and perverts who imperil the existence of the family and the common good.

CHOICE VS. DISCOVERY

Earlier, I devoted considerable discussion to the elements of human sexuality. It should be clear by now that *neither* homosexual nor heterosexual orientation is deliberately chosen, but both are acquired determinations over which the individual exercises little conscious direction. Homosexuality can be chosen only in the sense that men or women, recognizing their orientation, accept it and validate it by assuming a homosexual life-style, whether responsibly or not. Further, homosexuality is not contagious, nor can people be "converted" from heterosexuality to homosexuality. This means that past the end of the adolescent period of sexual development, a person's sexual orientation is not basically subject to major alteration, voluntary or involuntary.

Despite well-known claims of success, lasting sexual reorientation seems to be highly questionable in principle and fact, whether accomplished by behavioral modification, psychoanalysis or other forms of therapy. The exception appears to be cases of pseudohomosexuality, a form of homosexual fascination experienced primarily if not exclusively by heterosexual males, probably as compensation for feared sexual inadequacy or other deficiencies. Re-orienting a truly homosexual person is not only another matter, it is almost certainly doomed to failure, *even* among highly motivated "patients." Initial "successes" generally revert back to their fundamental orientation after a period of time. The lack of adequate follow-up studies further compromises claims of permanent change.[3]

How many gays and lesbians would want to change even if they could simply by "pushing a button," is not at all certain. What is certain, at least from my own interviews as well as other published accounts, is that very many would not.

Regarding the so-called danger of increasing the incidence of homosexuality by tolerance, anthropological research indicates that, despite wide differences in cultural attitudes, neither toleration nor suppression alters the basic incidence of homosexuality or homosexual behavior. Some of the most tolerant societies show the least incidence of both.

CAUSALITY

In terms of the "causes" of homosexuality, as we have seen earlier, homosexual preference is not traceable to a single cause or even to a typical pattern of causes, despite claims to the contrary. No known theory accounts for the facts in the majority of cases. Again, homosexuality is not an "all or nothing" state, but a *factor* which will be more or less predominant in all normal people, as well as one which varies in importance and strength, especially during the early phases of psychological development. Homosexual interest may be a transient stage in a person's life. It may well emerge late in

[3] Cf. Judd Marmor, M.D., "Homosexuality and Sexual Orientation Disturbances," in *The Sexual Experience,* Benjamin J. Sadock, Harold I. Kaplan and Alfred M. Freedman, eds., Baltimore: The Williams and Wilkins Co., 1976, pp. 374–91. See also the discussion of the works cited by Karlen, Churchill, Ovesey, Weinberg, Freedman and Hoffman.

life, even after decades of "dormancy." Generally, the dominant pattern is set early in life.

But to those for whom homosexual preference is the dominant and most continuous direction of "object choice," homosexuality is an existential "given" that can be accepted or rejected, but not "cured." The equation of homosexual feelings and experience with sickness is a barbarism we are all better off relegating to the moralistic, magical medicine of past ages. As a human condition, homosexuality may not in itself be designated a disease, according to the American Psychiatric Association, the American Psychological Association, and the National Institute of Mental Health. Therefore, speaking of "healing" people of homosexuality is an abuse of language . . . and persons.

PROMISCUITY

It is a commonplace that gays, especially men, are notoriously promiscuous. It is probably true that most homosexual liaisons among men, especially the young, are—like those of their heterosexual counterparts—unstable. That is, they are *intended* to be brief, noncommittal affairs of mutual enjoyment. But many, possibly most gay men and women also hope for a lasting relationship with one other person. And many in fact achieve their goal—far more than once believed by researchers (whose main avenue of information often lay through bars and baths). This is especially true of lesbians. But as gay men mature, they, too, tend to form more permanent relationships and "settle down."

Being personally acquainted with a number of gay and lesbian couples, some of whom have lived together for twenty years or more, I find the charge of instability to be one of the most unfortunate and unjust myths. The typical theological attitude in this regard is especially painful. For instance, a leading moralist recently wrote that permanent bonds rooted in deep interpersonal love between homosexual males are rare, but he conceded that in terms of an alternative lifestyle of promiscuity, such unions can be accepted as "a lesser evil." The irony consists in the fact that such unions have been roundly denounced by traditional moralists as the *greater* evil. Further, one of the reasons churchmen believe lasting gay unions to be rare is that those admitting to them have often been accused of living in sin, denied the sacraments as impenitent sinners, and sometimes literally driven out of the church. In terms of increasing promiscuity among gays, the church is not guiltless.

With an increased acceptance of gay unions by society and churchmen, there is good reason to believe that promiscuity will in fact decrease, contrary to current myth.

Casual and indiscriminate sexual encounters and lifelong "monogamous" relationships in fact represent extremes of a whole spectrum of gay relationships. Many close relationships are not genitally expressed at all. Others which find or are built upon sexual expression are relatively long-term affairs— from a few weeks or a month or two to a matter of years. But such relationships are not promiscuous in the customary sense of that word. From one perspective, these "unions" are facsimiles of a great many straight liaisons—minus the social and ecclesiastical rituals of serial bonding and splitting. From another viewpoint, these relationships are indeed "another kind of love"—affectionate, caring and responsible, neither promiscuous nor an ape of marriage. Being different from the classical pattern of heterosexual unions, these liaisons are difficult to categorize. Consequently moralists in particular are at a disadvantage in evaluating them. Surely one of the major tasks of the gay Christian community will be to explore such distinctive elements of gay experience, raising them to the level of critical consciousness in the light of the Gospel of Christ as well as the demands and unique situation of the gay world.

FAMILY VALUES

Finally, if not completely, it is a prevalent belief that homosexuality, or, more concretely, *gays* are dangerous to individuals, especially children, and to social values in general, especially those of the family. In *fact,* the vast majority of gay men and women are ethically conscientious, law-abiding and valuable members of society. Some criminals are homosexual

—apparently Babyface Nelson and John Dillinger were; most apparently are not. Sex-offenses involving true molestation of adults and children are committed by less than one percent of the homosexual population—a figure roughly equivalent to that of offenders in the heterosexual population, which is ten times larger. This simply means that nine out of ten sex-offenders, including child-molesters, are straight. (The sexual "crimes" gays—usually men—are accused of almost invariably involve the private activities of consenting adults, acts now legal in seventeen states and nearly every nation in the world. Lesser offenses typically include solicitation, loitering, and "disorderly conduct"—i.e., dancing in a gay bar.)

Regarding the family itself, some gays have experienced rejection and hostility from parents and relatives; others, tragically, have broken off all contact with their families, either out of fear of rejection or in order to spare their parents grief and suffering. But many gays retain excellent family relations, whether or not their homosexuality or their life-style is approved of. Many more would like to. Often, gay men and women devote years of their lives to the care of aged or infirm parents. Further, gays are increasingly petitioning to adopt children on the grounds that a child's having a homosexual parent (or parents) is preferable to having none. (There is no evidence that sexual orientation can be influenced simply by having a homosexual parent; presumably, most gays had straight parents.) Among other advantages natural or adopted children will probably receive from a gay parent is freedom from the scourge of homophobia. Thus, despite much sanctimonious scare-talk about increased acceptance of homosexuality weakening family ties, it is even more likely that a saner attitude in this respect will actually strengthen the family.

SEEING GAY

The primary means of destroying myths about gays and gay life is *looking:* For gays, looking into themselves honestly, willing to affirm the special qualities, talents, skills and interests that make each person unique, but also willing to ac-

knowledge their deficiencies and defects and to begin correct-
ing them where possible. Honest discernment also requires
looking carefully at the standardized life-styles which the gay
ghetto presents as efforts at self-actualization, then deciding
whether to fit into the stereotypes or risk becoming a "character." For straights, it means looking honestly at their own
prejudices, personal fears and attitudes. Even in the face of
obvious gay role-playing, straight persons should recall that
each human being is a distinct individual with a unique personality, talents, capacities and problems. The masks and
ruses straights encounter in the ghetto are often assumed because *they* have been the aggressor. . . .

The "problem" of homosexuality is primarily one of
straight liberation—liberation from the myths, stereotypical
thinking and the consequent forms of discrimination that, in
turn, engender defensive postures among gays. Disabusing
people of prejudicial notions can only be achieved, as I noted
before, by education, which thus becomes a tactical necessity
in any strategy for gay emancipation by both gays themselves
and concerned straights. Self-education is, again, a precondi-
tion for educating the straight world, a task especially important for teachers, counselors and clergy. (A few references
for further reading are listed in the epilogue.)

Gays can (and must) also do much in the witness of their
behavior to demonstrate the falsity of the myths and prejudices that demean them. Rather than coming out of the ghetto
defensively, this means coming out proudly and honestly,
willing to work and, if need be, to suffer in order to achieve a
more liberated society.

Chapter Four
LIVING IN A GAY WORLD

As do the members of any persecuted minority, many gay men and women gather together into somewhat protective groups for social purposes and sometimes for living in proximity. The creation of what many gays themselves call the "gay ghetto" is thus at least partially a consequence of society's hostility toward gays. And, as is true of any ghetto, the gay ghetto manifests the characteristic qualities of those who populate it—including both the most and least admirable traits.

Increasingly greater attention is being paid to the dual social context of homosexuality by psychologists and sociologists. (By "dual" I mean both the general heterosexual environment and the specifically homosexual milieu.) Theologians have been much slower to assess homosexual behavior in terms of social structures and dynamics. Consequently, most religious literature still focuses on individual acts, more often than not taken abstractly—the so-called "objective morality."

But society provides the foundation for all moral decisions and acts; understanding homosexuality thus demands a look at the gay ghetto as well as the influence of the straight world.

As a subculture, the gay world has its own language, customs, beliefs, values and institutions, rather sharply dichotomized along male-female lines in many instances. An element of conflict with many values in the dominant straight society also gives the gay world the character of a counterculture. Language, however, presents the clearest instance of the distinctiveness of gay society and also provides a useful index to important ideas, cultural patterns and values.

GAY TALK

Throughout the preceding chapters I have used terms such as "gay" and "straight," "homosexual" and "heterosexual," which, whether slang or technical are well-enough known not to warrant much elaboration. But for those readers unfamiliar with the language of the gay world, some clarification of the semantics involved will be helpful enough to justify a brief digression.

Gay is slang or "street talk" for homosexual, and often implies "male." It, too, is an adjective, but is used frequently as a noun. Obscure but ancient in origin, "gay" was often used of women as well as men of various sexual "persuasions" and occupations, usually suggesting a certain looseness of morals. Today, no specific moral judgment is implied, but in the gay world, the associations are favorable and the word is greatly preferred to technical terms such as "homosexual," "invert," etc. "Gay" often refers to life-style or to the whole homosexual subculture. It further designates persons who have accepted their homosexuality as an integral part of their personalities, and are privately and to a greater or lesser extent publicly comfortable being known as homosexual. In distinction from persons whose homosexuality is hidden, repressed or clandestine, gays are said to be "out of the closet." Often, being publicly "out" is expressed by direct political activity, but not all gays are militants or political activists.

Lesbian, which many homosexual women prefer to "gay," derives from the tradition that the great poetess, Sappho of Lesbos, was homosexual. She may or may not have been.

Straight is common jargon for heterosexual, both male and female, with the usual implication of exclusivity—a gross oversimplification. The "straight world" thus means everything not manifestly gay. "Straight" can also be used as a noun or an adjective.

Coming out refers to the recognition, acceptance and acknowledgment of homosexual preference, usually in terms of an actual temporal event. Being "brought out" means being sexually initiated into the gay world, usually by a more experienced partner; it does not refer to passing, single or child-hood experiences. "Being out" refers to the state of identifica-tion as gay, usually in some kind of public context. What gays are out *of* is "the closet," that is, the condition of secrecy. "Closet queen" is most often a term of mild contempt—less mild if a reference to a homosexual male who actively pre-tends to be heterosexual in order to avoid discrimination. ("Queen" or "quean" originally meant a female prostitute, but was later applied to homosexual men; today it especially refers to men who affect a regal and effeminate attitude.)

Lover usually means a more or less permanent, faithful sexual partner, as opposed to a "trick," a "number," or "trade" someone might encounter during a "one-night stand." (In general, these terms appropriately apply only to males.) "Tricking" means picking up a casual sex partner on a non-payment basis. Among gays, "trade" refers to a male, fre-quently claiming to be heterosexual, who seeks sex with a gay partner, but who refuses to perform any acts he construes to be "feminine." A "hustler" is a male prostitute who provides sexual services for men (as well as women) for money, but who also may not be homosexual himself. Many hustlers are also trade, that is, they will perform only what they consider to be the "male" role in sexual relations. Some hustlers are vicious thugs who prey on homosexual clients, beating and robbing them, sometimes resorting to blackmail and even to murder.

Cruising means street-walking, frequenting public lava-tories ("tea-rooms"), gay bars and other designated locales, or otherwise actively seeking to pick up someone interested in casual sex. It also refers to the visual scrutiny of a potential sex partner, sometimes including mutually provocative eye-contact.

Camp now means an ironic style of commentary or deport-ment, whether expressed in gestures, mannerisms, speech, dress or even decor. Once a theatrical term for exaggerated and effeminate speech, "camp" may have had its origins in the dense living arrangements of young gay actors during the Depression, many of whom banded together in "camps" for economic reasons. Today, it refers to almost any kind of haughty, hyperbolic innuendo, or even to a taste for the outrageous in clothing and furniture. "Camping" may seem (and often is) superficial and innocuous, but it often acquires a biting edge and evolves quickly into sarcasm. Although quick wit is almost a characteristic of the gay ghetto, not all gays are comfortable being "campy" because of the aura of effeminacy surrounding it.

Butch, which means masculine or *macho* is rapidly being taken over by chic straights; its correlative, *nelly,* meaning effeminate or "swishy," is by no means as common. *S & M* means sado-masochistic—in this context, homosexual activities that involve symbolic or actual physical violence or, more likely, extreme forms of sexual experience. *Chicken* means young, particularly someone (usually male) who is legally underaged or looks it.

Gay jargon employs dozens of other phrases to designate people, behavior, dress, attitudes, relationships and much more, most of which is either self-explanatory or not immediately relevant here. The special language of the ghetto serves many purposes: it ties gays together verbally, almost as if by code, often in the form of double-meanings and connotation. It thus serves also as an instrument of verbal exclusion against straights. Gay argot can also convey subtle shades of meaning only gays would understand or appreciate.

It should be noted here that the straight world also has its share of gay references—most of them highly pejorative: homo, queer, fairy, les, lesbo, faggot, fag, pansy, dyke, fruit, bugger, etc. Some of these terms were probably gay jargon at one time. Occasionally gays use them, much as blacks sometimes call each other "nigger" in a faintly deprecatory or censorious manner. Like blacks, gays understandably resent such terms when directed at them by outsiders. I am unaware of any words gays use to express the same kind of contempt, ridicule or antagonism toward straights as those listed above, or such as the black term "whitey" manifests. This may well indicate a far greater interest in, as well as a fear of, homosexuality than most heterosexual persons would care to admit to, as well as a curious lack of anti-straight sentiment among gays.

THE INVISIBLE WALL

As a more or less visible subculture, the gay world functions primarily as a social network, concretized in the form of several specifically gay institutions—the gay bar, the "baths," bookstores, theaters and arcades specializing in gay pornography. There are as well, gay restaurants, discos, barber shops, health clinics, counseling centers, newspaper offices, political headquarters and churches. Gay brothels have a long history. Gay-owned establishments, from art boutiques to haberdasheries either cater to gays or are given preferential patronage. "Software" tends to link the gay world together by magazines, newspapers, films, paperbacks and the "grapevine."

Except for the baths, what is distinctive about ghetto institutions is not so much their services, but their clientele, which tends to be exclusively gay and usually male. The lesbian ghetto is neither as extensive nor as public as its male counterpart. Some of the reasons for this include the greater overt persecution of gay men and, hence, the greater need for defensive association; the greater freedom of movement men traditionally enjoy in our culture; the greater wealth accessible to men; and the apparent preference of lesbians for private and domestic rather than public association. The sexual attraction that tends to bring men and women together in straight society is lacking, of course, in the gay world, which increases the separateness of the gay and lesbian ghettoes, although gay and lesbian friendships are not uncommon.

Typically, in the past, the lesbian and gay ghettoes overlapped only at the fringes; today, the greater political awareness and social solidarity of both groups encourages more exchange, a fact which indicates that the quest for sexual satisfaction is by no means the only glue holding the gay world together internally. As the struggle for liberation progresses, gay-lesbian association will probably increase, creating a unique opportunity for the emergence of inter-sexual relationships of an especially important character today: nonerotic friendships.

At present, however, the gay world is predominantly a

male-dominated one, perhaps even more than is the straight world. Thus, most of what I have to say about gay institutions applies primarily, if not only, to those catering to men. Some male institutions, such as the baths, are absent from the lesbian world, as far as I know.

Not all urban gays, in fact a minority, actually live in the gay ghetto, whether considered to be a territory or a culturally closed realm of shared interests and values, etc. The ghetto is nevertheless the nucleus of the gay world, to a greater or lesser degree shaping the attitudes of most gays, even those who live in rural areas. Communication is effective. Chains of baths across the country issue credit cards for travelers. Gay directories and bar guides provide access to gay areas of every major and many minor cities on a worldwide basis. Benevolent organizations such as One, Inc., the Daughters of Bilitis, Mattachine, the Metropolitan Community Church, Dignity and Integrity, as well as various Gay Liberation Fronts and alliances reinforce the gay social network in many different ways.

GAY BARS

Most homosexual persons—about nine out of ten, according to a 1968 study—have never seen the inside of one, but the gay bar has become the institutional symbol of the ghetto as the major recreational and social institution.[1] So successful are the bars, at least temporarily, that in larger cities "superbars" are opening which draw not only gay crowds in the hundreds, but almost as many straight customers, eager to capitalize on the farthest-out variety of "radical chic." A city the size of Los Angeles, New York or Chicago can support several superbars and as many as one hundred or more regular gay bars.

Most are pleasant places, more so than the majority of straight and even "singles" bars—less violent, more congenial, livelier and in better repair. Many have restaurants and discos attached. Some are intentionally raunchy, some syndicate-

[1] Cf. Wayne Sage, "Inside the Colossal Closet," *Human Behavior,* Vol. 4, No. 8 (August 1975), p. 16.

owned, others discriminate against straights or even other gays, depending on whether a bar caters to the S & M crowd, "cowboys," lesbians, blacks, Puerto Ricans or just males. Lesbian bars tend to be smaller and less elaborate than male bars, partly because fewer lesbians "make the bar scene," and partly because the real money and power in the gay world are in male hands.

The main function of the gay bar is to provide an open environment for drinking, mixing, cruising and often dancing and other forms of entertainment. Gay bars are, of course, moneymaking enterprises, most, apparently, doing very well.

Despite the positive contributions gay bars make to the lives of men and women who are often alone and lonely, they are first of all bars, and alcoholism becomes a serious problem for many gays as a result. Bars are also expensive as meeting places, as is any commercial establishment. Further, despite the recreational benefits bars provide, they are intended to be cruising grounds and thus contribute their share to the promiscuity that enervates the gay world. The pressure exerted by the need to appear young and attractive, in addition to the dynamics of "mating rites," sexual competition, frustration and loneliness, make the bars a highly mixed bag for gays attempting to create a life-style of integrity and dignity.

Given their detrimental effects, bars are still one of the less harmful institutions in the gay world. As bars, I might add, they are usually cleaner, friendlier and less expensive than equivalent straight establishments. In this respect, the gay world has probably had a redeeming effect on one of society's more troublesome institutions. The same can be said for discos, which in larger cities are becoming alternatives to bars alone as a social gathering place. In addition, gay discos are increasingly attracting straight couples, and even singles, who are looking primarily for a good atmosphere for dancing and mixing, and one free from the sexually competitive *Saturday Night Fever* syndrome.

THE BATHS

Gay steam baths are an integral part of the male ghetto,

whether the side attraction of run-down hotels which cater to transients, or superplush clubs featuring cafes, entertainment, saunas, massage, swimming pools, gyms and cocktail lounges. But in both cases, the purpose of the baths is the same: to provide a safe area for casual sexual encounters. Gay baths typically contain individual "cubicles" for customer enjoyment, usually a small room with a padded bench and a door, or at least a drape, which can be closed for the sake of privacy. Most baths also have one or several large "orgy rooms" for group activities.

From a Christian viewpoint, today's baths are as likely to be as detrimental to responsible sexuality as were those of the late Roman empire. Regardless of their harmless, even positive features, the baths promote promiscuity and sexual obsessiveness and, as well, feed off both. They are a major factor in the spread of venereal diseases.

I shall return later to the problems created for a Christian spirituality by some of the exploitative institutions which debilitate the gay ghetto from within. It is worth noting here, however, that there are worse things both in the gay world and outside of it than bars and baths—pharisaism for one. The baths at least provide a relatively humane escape for lonely, frustrated and rejected men, as well as the compulsive, timid and unattractive, and in this have a kind of social value. The tragedy lies in that the baths can never be more than a temporary expedient and especially in the fact that there are so few alternatives.

THE BUSHES AND BEACHES

Certain areas in cities and larger towns are generally well known by gays and many straights as cruising grounds—parks, stretches of beach, certain streets and parts of town, as well as railroad and subway stations, airports and bus terminals, where the public lavatories often provide available if risky rendezvous. Even in small towns, there is usually a "strip," where hustlers congregate, at least until the police force a relocation. In rural areas, there are gay taverns, not too far, as a rule, from major highways and usually known to interested parties from the general region. In small communities, individual gay homeowners may throw open their houses for meeting places.

Cruising the beaches and bushes is tricky business, not merely because solicitation is illegal. Chance meetings often terminate in ugly scenes of violence, occasionally even murder, as young hoodlums, desperate for drugs, liquor or just money, prey on men equally desperate for clandestine sex or just human contact. Hustlers, too, are sometimes beaten and even killed by psychopathic clients who vent their self-hatred on the spent object of their lust. The least risk is contracting one or another venereal disease, forms of which are pandemic in the gay world.

Beyond the physical dangers, there is also the human factor of degradation and exploitation that makes the bushes and beaches highly objectionable haunts for anyone capable of self-respect and love. The persistence of such places constitutes an indictment of the social pressures that create and support them.

ADDED ATTRACTIONS

Lesser institutions, if not unimportant in the lives of many gays, include movie theaters and night clubs where drag shows and female impersonators are featured, bookstores and cheap arcades, and, beyond the geographical sphere, newspapers and magazines. While by no means limited to gay audiences, especially the drag shows, the common element in most is more or less obvious pornography—the glorification of genital experience in all its forms, saving that of love and fidelity. Gay films in particular have so little redeeming value of any kind, *especially* artistic, that it is difficult to see in them anything but voyeuristic avenues of escapism and mindless visual prostitution.

CREATIVE ALTERNATIVES

Gay liberation groups, church organizations and associations such as Mattachine, which have their special place in the gay world, have criticized and sometimes even protested against the exploitative institutions in the ghetto. They have also attempted to develop alternatives to the bars, bushes and baths. Sports groups, bridge clubs, theater parties, discussion groups, picnics, tours and charter travel, dances and banquets and other creative and enjoyable activities have been sponsored and are usually well-attended, especially by those who find the bars unappealing.

While temporary by nature and less obviously successful than their competition, such optional activities are needed in the gay world not only for what they are not, but because of the wider experience, educational input and creative outlets they provide, enriching the gay community as a whole. Once again, as social acceptance increases and the need for protective association diminishes, such alternatives will become more important in terms of enhancing the solidarity and stability of the gay community. Needless to add, the bars and baths will survive, and with them the drag balls and "beauty contests," alcoholism and VD.

THE GAY WORLD

Gay society is a sieve of gossip and rumor, punctuated by jealousies, envy, spite, callousness, schemes for petty revenge, sarcasm, fickleness, deceit, disloyalty, promiscuity, shallowness, and sometimes violence. It is a world dominated by tight conventions, custom and style in everything from apparel, cosmetics and hair to rituals of dance, new drinks and topics of conversation. Outsiders are not usually welcome. Underlying everything are the subtle or gross patterns of mating games.

In short, the gay world is significantly like the rest of society, from small town Peyton Places to suburban and metropolitan communities bound together by human weakness, sin and culpability as much as by bonds of support, cooperation and celebration. Not just a subculture, the gay world is also a microcosm of society, manifesting in sharper relief the vices and virtues of the dominant culture, minus much of the bland in-between.

As a condensation of society, the gay world is also significantly rich in human values—intense loyalty, lasting friendships, trust, optimism and collaboration. Genuine love and companionship are not lacking, nor are humor and depth. But many critics and even sympathetic observers fail to detect the positive side of gay life because they are more distracted than gays themselves by the surface sexual tension and campiness evident in most gay haunts and habitats. Conversely, gays can become insensitive to the unpromising and destructive aspects of gay life by reason of familiarity.

There are dangers in the gay ghetto that are the price of the ghetto itself. The overall problem is engulfment—being smothered by a preoccupation with homosexuality and the consequent loss of contact with the straight world. Gays run a real risk of becoming insensitive to the values, life-struggle and needs of the great majority of people in the world by too exclusive a concentration on their own, thus reproducing the blindness that has prevented straight society from accepting gays. Microcosmic irony . . . .

But it is likewise important to recognize the positive functions of the gay ghetto—as a barricade against depersonalization and loneliness many gays find in the straight world in which they work and move, as an environment which permits honesty and openness about themselves, mutual acceptance and provides the opportunity for real friendships, some of life-long duration.

Chapter Five
GAY LIFE JOURNEYS

Such are the major institutions gays and lesbians encounter as members of the world's largest minority group, if they are socially active at all. The social structures of the gay world exert considerable pressure on gay men and women to conform to the expected patterns of participation in the ghetto. These same structures also establish the possibility of the association and solidarity requisite for psychological and spiritual integrity among such a socially dispossessed minority.

Three periods in a gay person's life stand out as particularly important regarding adjustments to these structures and pressures as well as the opportunities and problems they present: coming out, the crisis period and aging.

COMING OUT

The ability to recognize and accept one's homosexuality and to share that discovery with others marks a transition or "rite of passage" from the officially straight world to the gay world. For many young gays, the transition is easier today because of the greater receptiveness of their families and friends. For others, coming out is a crucifixion which can create disaster for family relations and elicit rejection from friends and acquaintances. Knowing this, some gays understandably but unfortunately never "get around" to telling even their closest friends and relatives about themselves, which means that they must live between two worlds, with the continual fear of discovery and mutual hurt.

Coming out is as much (or more) a psychological achievement as it is a merely historical moment in a person's life journey. For many, it is akin to a religious conversion. Once "out," they experience a tremendous sense of relief and well-being, a conviction of honesty and an exhilarating feeling of freedom. Frequently, however, the exuberance is short-lived, especially if coming out is associated with a deep plunge into the whirlpool of genital adventures especially open to the young. Sometimes a reaction of intense depression follows, a sense of loss and the fear that there is no going back but little by way of a future. Some highly sensitive teenagers and older gays as well may attempt suicide at this time, particularly when there has been an experience of familial rejection.

Not all gays come out as teenagers; most perhaps come out in their twenties and thirties, after college or as they take up a place in the work-a-day world. Some come out in middle or even old age, others after a marriage failure, others after the death of a spouse. In each case, coming out has its own character, whether easy and thrilling, slow and uneventful, or difficult and, later on, regrettable. The vast majority of gays never get all the way out of the closet, by the way. Their reasons are usually good ones; not everyone who resists being labeled does so out of fear. Coming out has problems associated with it that are not wholly the effect of a traditionally hostile society, but stem from the fact of labeling itself, whether done by oneself or by others. I shall return to the problem of labeling; here, it is enough to point out an important difference between being recognized and accepted as gay and the public proclamation of that fact.

If you are gay, psychologically and spiritually, coming out in the basic sense of self-acceptance and openness with significant others should be a constructive move, provided that you have sufficient inner strength and social support to carry through successfully. A half-hearted, experimental "try" can be permanently damaging to your own self-esteem and to your reputation among family members and associates.

Coming out without sufficient self-acceptance is an invitation to further problems. Needless to add, self-acceptance is not achieved in a single stroke of affirmation—it is a life-long process. By *sufficient* self-acceptance, I mean a fundamental sense of self-worth that can provide enough psychological stamina for you to survive rather severe challenges and opposition. From a religious point of view, it means a basic *moral assurance* that what you are is also the work of God, that you are following the route your conscience approves as your way to Christian maturity and lasting self-respect. It involves a willingness to be proved wrong, knowing that you can always do better and that a mistake need never be terminal. In this respect, coming out must be a part of your "fundamental option" for ultimate integrity and well-being as a friend of man, woman and God.

Before coming out, then, *be sure you're gay!* Today college and even high school experience provides ample opportunity for sexual experimentation. As a consequence, many young men and women may have as many or even more homosexual than heterosexual encounters, but without being thereby ready to or even capable of coming out for the simple reason that they are not really gay.

Considerable activity among adolescents goes on which is technically homosexual but no indication of constitutional homosexuality, much less pathology or even gross immorality. I am referring to activities such as some of the initiation rituals or hazing in clubs and fraternities, as well as "circle jerks" and other forms of mutual masturbation or simply the mutual exploration that goes on among children.

Some youngsters who participate in same-sex games will eventually come out gay, but others, *most* others, will not. This is no indication that the first group is "fixated," nor that the second is "latent"—conditions that are both highly mythological. Counselors should be alert to the *variety* of possible directions sexual orientation may take in a young person's life; experiences at any one period of development cannot be taken as representative of the entire process nor indicative of the outcome. Sexual identity is not complete, in all likelihood, until the middle twenties, even though most gay and straight adolescents will be well aware of the predominant direction of their sexual interests by the time they are sixteen or seventeen. Some kinds of sexual experimentation, including homosexual experiences, must be considered as falling within the normal range of adolescent behavior. The morality of such behavior must be judged accordingly.

To repeat, *the capacity to respond sexually to a person of the same gender is not equivalent to being homosexual.* In this sense, *gay* means a predominant sexual attraction to persons of the same gender with a proportionate and constitutional lack of attraction to members of the opposite gender. The number of men and women who have had homosexual "experiences" but have gone on to happy and successful lives as husbands, wives and parents *far outweighs* the number whose sexual preference and experience are exclusively gay or straight. Integrating such experiences into a balanced sexual history can contribute to human wholeness; denying them, trying to "forget" them, or worrying about them for years merely present occasions for needless self-deprecation.

Similarly, given the fundamental homosexual *capacity* in every one of us, the emergence in consciousness of homosexual attraction or even genital arousal should not be an occasion for panic. It is likely that most straight men and women will sometimes experience strong attractions like these, even after marriage. Neither panic, flight nor a total capitulation to homosexual infatuation are mature responses. But if the situation is met adequately, that is with honesty and restraint, greater self-awareness and the growth of valuable and lasting relationships will most likely result.

For a husband or wife who experiences recurrent homosexual "crushes," fantasies or finds himself or herself involved in a homosexual affair, skilled counseling is warranted. If a professional counselor is unavailable, talking things over calmly with one's spouse, an understanding pastor or trusted friend *may* help. But resolutely hiding the situation will not. While true bisexuality (equal or similar attraction to members of both sexes) is relatively rare, it apparently does exist, whether as a lasting condition or as a transient stage of development. Unlike constitutional homosexuality, I believe that such bisexuality need not invalidate a marriage, provided that both partners are able to cope with the situation maturely. Making a marriage successful in such a situation requires immense dedication, love and discipline. But it can be done.

Both research and pastoral experience indicate that the number of homosexual men and women in heterosexual marriages is much higher than might be expected. It may well be that even a majority of the actual homosexual population is thus married. A priests' survey conducted recently for the Thomas More Association indicated that 35 percent of those asking for pastoral help for a homosexual problem were married; 24 percent had children.[1] Attempting to generalize from the experience of troubled persons tends to unbalance the issue on the side of sickness and tragedy—as seen in the work of many psychiatrists and counselors such as the otherwise sympathetic treatment of Fr. Marc Oraison.[2] One legitimate conclusion from such a survey seems to be that heterosexual marriage and some degree of homosexuality are not absolutely incompatible, despite problems. Further, many of these marriages would be considered successful by ordinary standards of evaluation in our society. On the other hand, many gay men and women feel trapped in marriages by the force of social and religious pressure and are, in fact, living a lie. Honesty, justice and plain mental health call for a serious and sincere confrontation in this case, probably requiring the dissolution or annulment of the marriage.

At present, few counselors in high school or college, much less the family doctor or minister are sufficiently skilled to aid a young person or an older one in resolving problems of sexual orientation. At the minimum, it is crucial to find an advisor who is neither prejudiced against homosexuality as such nor a gay propagandist. Responsible counseling services, some of which specialize in sexual identity crises, can be located through referral by organizations such as One, Inc., Mattachine, the Daughters of Bilitis, and local chapters of Dignity, Integrity and the Metropolitan Community Church and so forth. (See the "postlude" for addresses.)

[1] Statistics compiled by the Thomas More Association, 180 N. Wabash Ave., Chicago, Ill. 60601, for publication in the newsletter *For Priests,* March 1977, No. II.
[2] Cf. *The Homosexual Question,* New York: Harper & Row, 1977. Oraison's treatment reflects his pronounced and somber existentialism as much as it does the fact that his experience has been admittedly limited to disturbed clients.

Ideally, coming out should be achieved in the context of a well-integrated relationship with those whom you choose to share this important part of your life with. For most gays, especially the young, there will be a desire to share the fact of the gayness with close friends and especially with their families. Older gays frequently want to include their close business associates or co-workers—an important step in so far as work relationships today are often some of the most significant in our lives. It may well be that they wish to include their pastor, doctor, lawyer and other personal associates. Some will want to tell the world. . . .

Here, common sense, courtesy and compassion will have to enter. Not everyone is likely to be ready for your announcement as soon as you are. The wider the intended audience, the greater the risk of misunderstanding and rejection, the more complex other repercussions. Each situation should be judged according to its own merits and context, and not merely in terms of your desire to be open. Enthusiasm can easily engender insensitivity.

However you decide to announce your gayness, respect, sincerity and concern must guide the announcement. If you have had the good fortune to receive counsel from an understanding minister, teacher or other trusted adult, it may well help to have him or her present when you meet with your parents—or children, wife or husband, for that matter. Other situations must be handled with similar care. Generally, when dealing with friends and acquaintances outside the immediate family group, it is wise to work from a foundation of achieved—not *presumed*—trust and respect. Premature self-disclosure can foreclose further opportunities for acceptance and mutual growth. Similarly, coming out aggressively, as punishment, retaliation or merely to wound someone in anger or, as is sometimes the case, striking back in pain, is at best childish, and more likely manipulative and cruel. "My mother made me gay," despite Bieber, Jung and toilet wall graffiti, is probably false and at best a gross oversimplification, but vastly effective as a weapon to demolish a parent already anxious about her "mistakes" in child-rearing. Coming out, if used to exonerate oneself and incriminate others is evidence of a precarious mental attitude; it is, simply speaking, a game: "See what you made me do?"

Parents, friends, relatives and co-workers of a gay person may often need more help to adjust than the gay "deb." Having a gay son or daughter is taken as a sign of personal failure; many close friends seem to fear guilt by association or even being contaminated.

Compassion and a better knowledge of the health in homosexuality should make such fears decrease, but they will probably never vanish, so long as human beings remain as mysterious and threatening to themselves as they are to each other. But if *your* child or parent or friend wishes to tell you that he or she is gay, be aware that this is probably an expression of confidence and trust from a person whose felt needs and vulnerability are at least as acute as yours, and who needs your respect, love and support more than anything in the world at that moment. Coming out should not be a personal disaster for anyone, nor a family crisis, the occasion for self-recriminations and accusations. All things considered, everyone is better off when gays are comfortably out of their restrictive identity-closets and accepted as gay—not coddled, pitied or even tolerated (which is demeaning and patronizing)—just simply *accepted*.

Acceptance is not *enough*, of course. But self-acceptance and immediate social acceptance are far more important than public proclamations. Without such acceptance as a foundation of support, public identification will likely be a precarious adventure into the social dynamics of labeling and "deviance." With acceptance, public declarations may well be unnecessary. Nevertheless, such political coming out often serves a positive purpose in changing general attitudes as well as exponentially raising the vital sense of self-worth among talented, constructively aggressive gays.

Many of the public utterances of liberated gays—"Gay is good," "Gay Power!" and "Out of the closets, into the streets!"—call to mind the slogans generated by the emergence of black power and the feminist movements: "I am somebody!" "Black is beautiful!" The startled and antagonistic reactions from liberal as well as more conservative quarters in the political, psychological and theological establishments which greeted these outbursts of "I'm OK" enthusiasm by men and women long conceded to be far from OK were also reminiscent of the not too distant past.

Whether true, mythical or just wishful thinking, the positive assertion of health and worth and dignity on the part of gays, however exaggerated or rhetorical, is a necessary and constructive phase of the dialectic of acceptance. Such claims do not in themselves *constitute* health, much less acceptability, but they help create conditions for providing both in a highly effective way. Affirmative slogans become problematic only if, behind a screen of propaganda, they obscure to straights or gays themselves the depths of pain and struggle involved in being gay.

Whether or not the slogan "Gay is good" sets your teeth on edge, and no matter how absurd the riders "Gay is better," "Gay is best," the fact remains that gays are good. The real point of coming out, however, is not to inform the straight world who is gay, but to secure a sense of valid personal identity and integrity.

THE CRISIS PERIOD

Being young is probably valued more in the gay world than in any other segment of society. Consequently, adolescence is typically extended to the utmost limits of credibility and aging is postponed (and feared) proportionately. The crisis period in the lives of many gays, then, is "the hump"—a period somewhere around thirty years of age, after which it becomes more and more difficult to pass as twenty-one, though many try.

The mid-years, with the transition phases of crises of limits, menopause and the male climacteric, plus the need for self redefinition in terms of personal and career opportunities, begin earlier in the gay world than in its straight counterpart, mainly because of the higher premium placed on youth, good looks and physical fitness. Handsome, youthful men and attractive, slim young women have more to lose with the passing of youth than their less well-endowed peers. Many cling feverishly to every vestige of adolescence, succumbing only resentfully to advancing maturity—which threatens them with loneliness, wrinkles, grey hair (or no hair), the loss of vitality, sociability, and the inevitable slowing toward the darkness of old age and death.

As "middlescence" approaches, many lesbians are especially tempted to "let go," meeting the so-called ravages of time with grim surrender rather than graceful acceptance. As with the aging male, lesbians at this period of life, particularly those who do not have a lover, need and should receive a great deal of support and encouragement—but not nagging or pampering. For in the difficult throes of this second radical challenge to self-affirmation, gays and lesbians themselves must appropriate the positive values and goals that will bring meaning and satisfaction to the closing years of their lives.

Handling acute depression, which sometimes accompanies the physiological and psychological changes at this period of life for *both* men and women, requires expert assistance. Although skilled helpers sensitized to the special needs of gay people are still greatly lacking, they are slowly increasing in number and professional competence. But a therapist insensitive to the unique needs of gays can do immeasurable harm by a mistaken attack on a sexual orientation. Gay "specialists" are devoting greater attention to the dynamics of the mid-years crises and aging, though by no means on a wide-enough scale.

Middle age is a time of life for many gays when the confines of the gay ghetto are too narrow; one of life's great discoveries as a person matures is the potential of human fulfillment on levels of interest and enjoyment that transcend youthful preoccupations and sexual differences. Wider social and cultural activities become, therefore, especially rewarding as gays and lesbians cross over "the hump." Many break out of the ghetto at this point—one reason why older men and women are not conspicuous in the bars and a more positive one than the mere fact of being older.

Although there are many common elements in gay and straight experiences and relationships, communication, intimacy and aging present particular stresses and problems for gays just as they have features not typical of heterosexual relationships. So, while gay persons can benefit greatly from counseling experiences, human relations workshops, and even books on personality development and interpersonal growth that are designed primarily for the straight world, there is a special need for gay counseling, seminars and resources. Surely one of the areas gay service organizations and religious groups should continue to emphasize, even increasingly so, is that of personal growth through shared experiences conducted by trained supervisors. Liberation is only the beginning of a meaning-filled, creative and developing life.

"AGING GAILY"

As has become clearer with each workshop and seminar with that title, after gays get past "the hump" they often begin to relax and to enjoy life more rather than less. Male gays in their forties and thereafter are more likely to follow the pattern of their lesbian sisters, find a lover and "settle down." (The number of "unions" among male gays is much higher than the myth allows even many gays to believe; serial monogamy is more the rule than a permanent relationship with a single person, but lasting relationships are not uncommon, even among younger gays.) Most "aged" gays I know, far from being bitter, lonely and depressed, are remarkably contented men and women. Social research seems to be increasingly confirming this and similar observations.

Older gays are often spared some of the more difficult trials of their straight counterparts—the disruption of the family, being forgotten or relegated to a "home" by one's own children, the gradual loss of contact with children and grandchildren. For lovers, however, age brings its losses to both gays and straights alike—the gradual disappearance of friends, the inevitable loss of one's life-companion, the smaller diminishments of dwindling income, strength and health.

Advanced age need not be a period of loneliness, even for single or "widowed" gays, however; the greater solidarity of the gay world provides social contacts and opportunities for sharing often denied straight persons. I have often been amazed and gratified to see the consideration and attention young gays show their elder brothers and sisters as well as their own aged parents and relatives. Older gays seem, as well, to acquire a sense of detachment not only from the gay world, but from the world in general which I cannot help but see as a religious response to the developing awareness of life's beauty and meaning. Nevertheless, they also preserve a sense of care and interest in people and the two worlds they live in that exceeds that of far younger people.

Such observations are, of course, limited and hardly applicable to all older gays. But they are indicative of the possibilities there for all. . . .

Throughout your life, if you are gay, it *is* possible to enjoy a sense of well-being and personal dignity that will bring you to the end of your days a happy and peaceful man or woman, despite the many difficulties and setbacks that inevitably will come. Having met a good many elderly gays over the past six years, I can say that with some assurance, which I hope the parents and friends of gays will find encouraging. Successfully negotiating the perils of "the hump" and relishing the long slope down the other side of thirty requires discipline, however—the strenuous art of refusing to identify yourself with the surface realities of being gay, while affirming yourself as a loved and lovable person chosen by God for his own reasons to follow a life-way toward Home *as* a gay person.

Chapter Six
LIVING WITH THE CHURCH

"About a month ago, I went to the 'Winter Carnival' with a friend of mine. Saw the Dignity booth and both of us being Catholic walked over to it and picked up some literature. I suggested to my friend that we should go to St. Aelred's some Sunday as it would be a 'decent place' to meet people. We finally went last Sunday . . .

"I had an unexpected surprise. We were trying to participate in the service. I was standing in church attempting to sing when all of a sudden I wanted to cry, it felt so good to be participating in a Mass again. I choked back the tears because I didn't want my friend to laugh at me. I had a good warm feeling inside me. I still do. I suppose I have returned to the Church or will more fully as time goes on. It's really strange—I went to church to meet people and I think I've been reintroduced to the One I least expected to meet. I went to Mass last night for the sake of going to Mass, not to meet people."

The experience of the thirty-six-year-old man who wrote these words is not a rare one among the many gay men and women who have "come back" to the church through the programs and witness of Dignity, the Metropolitan Community Church, Jewish congregations such as Los Angeles' Metropolitan Community Temple, Bet Chayim Chadashim—"the house of new life," and other groups. What is remarkable is that they do come back, given the traditional religious hostility toward gays and lesbians. Some, of course, never left: "I remained because of a firm background understanding of the message of love in the Gospel. . . . I was able with the help of a good advisor to distinguish between the letter and the spirit of the law." A woman of forty-six wrote, "I have remained within our church because of an understanding young priest at our parish." A man of fifty-one explained simply, "I have never left the church and have always remained in it because I don't think there is any better."

Despite some hostility and bitterness toward an institution traditionally opposed to any manifestation of homosexuality as contrary to God's law and nature itself, vast numbers of gays and lesbians continue to revere the church and to desire to be full members—but not necessarily as celibates. Not a few churchmen are beginning to agree that they may have a case.

Although practice has often departed from theory in the pastoral ministry as well as in the private lives of priests, ministers, popes and rabbis, homosexuality has been considered a serious deterrent to a full religious life, if not an abomination worthy of death, by most western religious traditions. In England, St. Anselm apparently prevented the promulgation of anti-homosexual laws in the year 1102 as contrary to papal decree. And at that time, the English church may not have considered homosexual acts gravely sinful.[1] But the more general practice of the church's ministers, officially at any rate, has been to ban and even burn offenders, and not the least of their harshness has been expressed in the penances dealt out in the confessional. An evident favorite of several confessors in one Chicago parish was requiring penitents to wash their mouths out in the urinal of a public lavatory in the church. (Having been told this on various occasions by at least a half-dozen different men, I am inclined to accept it as a true account, although at first, I could not bring myself to believe it.)

While not a typical penance, similar atrocities are not uncommon in the devotional life of gays. I have heard several accounts of actual physical abuse, whether a confessor shouting at a penitent in the confessional of a crowded church, or even pulling a teenager out of the "box" and striking him.

[1] I am indebted here to the unpublished research of Dr. John Boswell of Yale University. Cf. also Arno Karlen, op. cit., p. 86.

Protestant ministers have read gays out of church publicly, following supposedly "private" conferences. A young man of twenty-six relates: "While on my high school retreat during my senior year, I told a priest about my being gay, although at the time I was not actually a practicing gay. He read me up one side and down the other, chewed me up and spit me out at much louder tones than a normal talking voice. When I walked back into the room, all heads turned and looked at me, or at least I thought so. That caused eight years' separation between the church and myself."

From a pastoral viewpoint, the possibility of a reconsideration of the church's teaching is less immediately important than a revision of *practice*—specifically the cruel and unusual punishments doled out to gays by confessors, ministers, boards of elders, synods, and preachers. A closer look at the sources of the traditional teachings may well speed that process along, however.

SCRIPTURE AND TRADITION

A lengthy study of scriptural and theological texts is far beyond even the intention of this essay, and probably unnecessary. A brief overview should explain why.

The Jewish and Christian tradition of opposition to homosexuality rests on several biblical texts. Most of the oldest deal with cult prostitutes (*kedeshim*) and need bother us no further (e.g., Dt. 22:5; I Kings 14:24; II Kings 23:7; Hosea 4:14, etc.). The important texts which concern us are Gen. 19:4–11, the story of Sodom and Gomorrah, a parallel story in Judges 19:16–30, and two accounts from the Holiness Code of Leviticus, 18:22 and 20:13; the last text alone mentioning the death penalty.

The traditional association of Sodom and Gomorrah with homosexual vice has been subject to recent criticism on scriptural grounds based on other references which do not even allude to homosexuality as the cities' crime (e.g., Is. 1:9–10; Jer. 23:14; Lk. 10:12, Rev. 11:8, etc.). Of some twenty-two biblical references, only three seem to indicate homosexual immorality, yet none make explicit mention of it (Ezek. 16:46f; II Peter 2:6 and Jude 7). But even if the cities' immediate provocation was attempted homosexual rape, that would not provide a basis for condemning all homosexual acts. Heterosexual rape was also an abomination to the Jews, especially when a violation of the law of hospitality, a point clearly made in the story of the Levite in Judges 19 (cf. also Dt. 22:25f.).

Rape is not at issue, however, in the passages from Leviticus, which are concerned with ritual purity and family integrity. But even here it is not all that clear that the "separateness of Israel" was not more important in the mind of the priestly writers than the specific malice of homosexuality. However that may be, the message is plain: "You shall not lie with a male as with a woman. . . ."

The phrase "as with a woman" appears in both texts and should be considered carefully. Here, as in the New Testament accounts, the writings of the Fathers and the great medieval theologians, it is apparent that (male) homosexuality is taken to be a voluntary perversion of the natural sexual instinct. To the ancient Judeo-Christian world, homosexual behavior involved a free choice to counter one's own nature and thereby the nature of human procreation itself, especially by recourse to cult prostitutes, which added the malice of idolatry. The question of constitutional homosexuality never came up at all.

In the New Testament, except for the references to Sodom and Gomorrah in II Peter and Jude, homosexuality is mentioned only three times, all in the Pauline writings. In Romans 1:26ff, where Paul is railing against idolatrous pagan worship, he does not use the word for homosexual which appears in I Cor. 6:9 and I Tim. 1:9–10 (*arsenokoitēs*). The context in Romans is apparently one of cult prostitution, as was that of most Old Testament references. Such a thing, he insists, represents the tragic legacy of idolatry.

The two other texts containing the Greek word for male homosexual appear in standard lists of sins. Significantly, no further references appear in the ten other lists in the Pauline writings, the four lists in other writings nor in the gospels. But there is no more reason in these two passages than in Romans to suppose that the author had anything else in mind than heterosexual indulgence in homosexual acts. Further, the scant biblical references to homosexuality *in general* seems to indicate that it was hardly a preoccupation of Paul or any other writer. Nor have these few texts been interpreted by the church as a total condemnation of homosexual persons, which would amount to a very un-Christian attitude. Rather, the meaning of the lists is that such acts, being immoral by definition, cannot characterize members of the Kingdom. But Paul could have had no knowledge of constitutional homosexuality; for him, homosexuality could only represent a deliberate perversion of heterosexuality. As such, homosexual acts *are* immoral. (The church's long recognition that true antecedent homosexuality invalidates marriage can also be argued to mean that for a true homosexual to attempt heterosexual acts is similarly immoral.)

The equally hostile polemics against perversion and institutionalized homosexuality by the Greek Fathers are well known and were probably well-taken. I am sure that St. John Chrysostom and Augustine would fulminate against the baths today as they did 1500 years ago, and for the same reasons. The great medieval theologians were likewise concerned with homosexuality as a perversion of heterosexual inclination as well as institutionalized vice. This tradition has continued to the present, generally following their lines of argumentation. However, much of their case is debatable on grounds similar to those which call into question the scriptural and patristic condemnations: an understandably inadequate grasp of human physiological and psychological development as well as woefully scant information about animal behavior, upon which much of their case rested.

But what we must concern ourselves with today is what Paul, John Chrysostom and Aquinas did not know: that true homosexuality is not a willful decision to "give up" heterosexuality, nor do most homosexual men and women lead lives of wild sensuality and irresponsible lust.

Constitutional homosexuality is a relatively recent discovery, psychologically speaking. The distinction between "innate" and "acquired" homosexuality was first seriously proposed in 1863, and, although the notion of congenital homosexuality has been abandoned, since the time of Freud, scientific thought has tended to accept constitutional homosexuality as a predominant, irreversible orientation acquired through a long developmental process beginning in early infancy, over which the individual has minimal control. Homosexual persons are neither born nor made; they are constituted.

Constitutional homosexuality, then, has not been dealt with in scripture, in traditional theology, nor even in the recent Vatican document on sexual ethics, which in its three "divisions" of transient, innate and pathologically constitutional homosexuality overlooked the largest class of all: the healthy homosexual population.

Erroneous beliefs about astronomy, biology and paleontology have not outdated the message of salvation recorded in the Bible; nor should the need to incorporate the accurate findings of psychologists and sociologists occasion fear about compromising the essential morality of the Judeo-Christian heritage. Christian gays, as we shall see, neither accept nor promote a double standard of morality.

Present theological opinion on the status of homosexuality is varied. Some moralists maintain or imply that homosexuality and heterosexuality are on equal footing ethically and psychologically, being alternative forms of human sexuality. The traditional Christian position holds that homosexuality represents an intrinsic disorder and can in no wise fulfill the meaning of human sexuality. While not a sinful state as such, any deliberate behavior expressive of that condition would be sinful. At best, homosexual "unions" are a "lesser evil" than outright promiscuity or compulsive behavior, but nevertheless represent an objectively sinful situation and may not be approved of directly.[2]

My own opinion is that both approaches miss the point. Given the complex and systemic nature of human sexuality,

[2] The most recent authoritative statement on homosexuality is found in the "Declaration on Sexual Ethics" (*Persona Humana*) issued by the Sacred Congregation for the Doctrine of the Faith and available through the Publications Office of the United States Catholic Conference, Washington, D.C., along with various commentaries from the Vatican newspaper, *L'Osservatore Romano*. A traditional psychological approach espousing this viewpoint can be found in John R. Cavanaugh, M.D., *Counseling the Homosexual*, Huntington, Indiana: Our Sunday Visitor Press, 1977.

he complementarity of male and female *persons* (not organs) in terms of psychological, physiological and sociological considerations means that heterosexuality constitutes
he common and normal, and therefore normative, condition
n which human persons can realize their sexual potential
most completely. Further, heterosexual intercourse is the nor-
nal and (for the foreseeable future) *only* way in which the
uman race is propagated (and even overpropagated). Homosexuality obviously differs from this *ideal* situation; techni-
ally, it is a deviation. Thus it is neither simply an alternative
or is it an abnormality in the sense of a pathological condi-
on, which is clear from the clinical evidence of persistent
nd extensive health among homosexual men and women de-
pite their "minority" status. Rather, homosexuality consti-
ites a *variation* within the normal range of human sexual
ifferences. As such it is a natural variation, not a sickness or
fault or a psychological, physiological or sociological aber-
ation, although any of these may accompany homosexuality
individual cases.

The fact of homosexuality may well arise because of some
spect of the "brokenness of the world" (Marcel). But be-
ause of that, it is not simply to be reckoned a "natural evil"
longside congenital defects and birth accidents. For homo-
exuality is not congenital, a defect or an accident, but an
cquired difference in sexual orientation which is multi-causal
nd has many possible manifestations. Further, the differ-
nce between heterosexuality and homosexuality in behavioral
rms is a matter of degree rather than a sharp divergence, as
knowledgeable writers affirm.

Asserting the moral superiority, inferiority or equality of
e varieties of human sexuality is therefore pointless, espe-
ally in concrete cases. Many homosexual relationships are
doubtedly superior to many heterosexual marriages, and
ce versa. However, in terms of the commonly accepted
lues of human society and Christian culture, heterosex-
lity clearly remains the ideal condition for men and
omen, as John McNeill himself implies.[3]

Nevertheless, even though a less-than-ideal "given" of the
man condition, homosexuality persists as a stable factor in

[3] McNeill, *The Church and the Homosexual*, p. 160. But see p. 122f.

all human cultures. As such a "standard deviation," it too is normative, or rather, para-normative. Further, it possesses a positive place and function in human experience. That is, it fits into God's "mysterious plan" for the salvation of the human race—both in the lives of particular persons and regarding the history and welfare of the human race. It is not a disease to be eradicated or a fault to be forgiven, but an opportunity for men and women to grow and develop into mature, loving and responsible human persons—*whether gay or straight.* Moreover, as part of the meaning of human experience, homosexuality has been taken up and redeemed by the incarnational transformation of human nature by the Word of God. Thus homosexuality contributes a dimension to human life without which our history and destiny on this planet would be far poorer.

Even beyond that, I believe that for individual persons and for the race, homosexuality has a positive meaning of its own, aspects of which I shall later attempt to describe. Most fundamentally, I see it as the revelation of the possibility of friendship among men and women of both the same and the opposite sexes based not upon biological differences or attraction but rather on psychological and sociological complementarity and spiritual attraction. As a redemptive dimension of human sexuality, homosexuality can help to heal the wounds inflicted on humanity by inter- and intra-sexual competitiveness. To borrow a phrase from Henri Nouwen, the gay person can be the "wounded healer" by whose stripes the potentially fatal aggressiveness of our race finds its cure by being transformed into the co-operativeness of true friendship.

ON CURING

As mentioned earlier, it is still a current belief among many churchmen that homosexuality represents a decision or a sickness and can be voluntarily reversed or cured. For instance, despite evidence that there is only a small likelihood of "substantial change" in sexual orientation past adolescence, plus resistance even to the thought of changing, on the basis that a reorientation of sexual preference is not *impossible,* one established and liberal moral theologian has recently written that change-therapy should nevertheless be advised for gays "whenever possible." He even admits that it will probably fail. In other words, gays should be advised to devote considerable amounts of time, emotional energy and, not least of all, money to an almost certainly hopeless quest before resigning themselves to the fact that "nothing more can be done." Then they may be advised to adopt a celibate lifestyle, or, if that is deemed impossible, permitted to continue receiving the sacraments even if in a "gay marriage," which is considered a lesser evil than a life of casual promiscuity.

Considering the sometimes permanent damage done to the self-esteem, hope, trust and budget of docile gays by psychiatric change-artists and behavioral mechanics, as well as the statistically established improbability of any positive change to begin with, such advice seems peculiarly antiquated and even heartless.

It would seem to me that before a confessor, advisor and, indeed, a gay client consider any scheme to change sexual orientation, thus tampering with the deepest wellsprings of human personality, they should possess *moral certitude* that there is a good chance of success, given 1) the person's desire and ability (including financial) to undergo long months if not years of therapy or analysis, 2) some evidence that there is sufficient heterosexual experience or at least interest to warrant such an endeavor, that is, that the person is not merely seeking to escape the difficulties and pain of being gay, and 3) the availability of an experienced therapist who will not violate the human dignity of his client and who is sufficiently skilled to be able to distinguish and deal with the client's nonsexual problems, which may not only be serious but need prior attention.

A further caution: the advisor's, confessor's or parent's (or whosever) animosity to homosexuality and anxiety to see gays "straighten out" are *never* sufficient reason to advise or demand change-therapy; the penitent's or client's needs, desires, conscience and capacities *must* come first, if not in the name of justice and compassion, at least in the name of professional competence.

Many psychiatrists and therapists, following Hooker, Tripp, Weinberg, Hoffman and others, are beginning to balk at the idea of exacting monetary and other sacrifices from gays merely to attempt the unlikely task of altering their sexual orientation. Several have publicly denied the possibility of changing the orientation of a constitutionally homosexual person without serious and perhaps lasting personality damage. Some argue that so-called "successes" do not constitute change so much as temporary diversions or the lasting suppression of all sexual interest, the psychological equivalent of castration.

These dissidents from the long-standing presumption that homosexuality is a choice or an illness that can be reversed or cured are apparently growing in numbers and influence in the world of psychology. Significantly, even Freud, who distinguished between neurotic and nonneurotic ("healthy") homosexuality, was pessimistic about efforts to redirect sexual preference—a step into the twentieth century that churchmen may someday follow.

FAITH HEALING

Presently, however, a small but evidently increasing number of clergymen, not content to rant against gays or command them to seek a cure, have themselves undertaken to heal them or their "plight," whether defined as sickness or sin. While an improvement over the stake and flames, such an approach is hardly less objectionable than (and not much different from) that of the gay-changing psychiatrists and aversion therapists.

While not ruling out a miraculous displacement of someone on the heterosexual-homosexual continuum (in either direction), I have my doubts about the condition of homosexual Christians "healed" in prayer meetings and exorcisms. The virtually total omission of follow-up on these "cases," as well as the general lack of criteria for determining what constitutes a cure raise serious questions about the truth of any claim and also about the morality of the attempts. From direct observation, I am not sure whether the last state of the victim not worse than the first—an innocuous if unhappy young gay now professes to be healed and "straight," yet continues frequent the baths and "tea-rooms." Even an unhappy gay is preferable to a schizoid one. . . .

In many instances religious healing for gays is not only desirable but, I think, possible; several I know have benefitted from such a ministry. I am referring to a healing of memories, reconciliation with parents and other family members, an alleviation of guilt and self-doubt and an improvement in the quality of human relationships from one of resentment, exploitation and possessiveness to one of effective compassion, service and encouragement toward growth and freedom. For some gays, such healing in their lives may lead them to a celibate life-style, or perhaps to a life of commitment in fidelity and constancy with another person. It will not, I am confident, make a gay or lesbian straight—although, as with psychotherapy, pseudo-homosexual reactions may well be alleviated for disturbed heterosexual persons.

The real spiritual healing gays so often desperately need is the grace of self-acceptance and affirmation; were faith healers to begin with an understanding of their potential for help in this area, their ministry of healing would take on a more truly humane and thereby a more Christian tone.

MORALITY

Many gays seem caught up in the same trap as the teaching church on the grass-roots level, one made more acute (and more important as a dimension of the prophetic character of Christian gays) by its dual force: first, the elevation of sexual behavior to an all-important position in life, and, second, the consequential tendency to relate to oneself and others primarily as sexual "objects" or merely objects—members of the opposite sex, unattractive and older persons, etc. Such a sexualization of existence is fraught with problems for gays as it has been for Christians in general. Sexual behavior becomes a field of excessively heightened moral consciousness, either so dominating morality as practically to become synonymous with it, especially with regard to sin and guilt, or eventually assuming practical independence from ordinary morality. Some gays (and straights) go so far in reaction as to reject the validity of any sexual norms and values applicable to either group, perhaps denying even the possibility of sinful sexual behavior short of rape and child-abuse.

Such a reactionary attitude is self-defeating. For the realm of sexuality is one of the most sensitive, fundamental and humane dimensions of life—if, indeed, *only* one. Thus it must include reference to moral values, norms and even etiquette that are subtle, perhaps delicately so, as well as profound. Further, and for the same reason, sexual morality cannot be taken as a paradigm for the rest of life's concerns, any more than sexuality can be regulated by some simple, all-encompassing ethic. The moral aspects of sexuality are special and important, but not *all*-important. Moral theologians as well as the gay-in-the-street can fall into the same trap of sexual obsession.

Because of the integrity of both human life and the Christian gospel, sexuality and its moral aspects must nevertheless be taken as *part* of life and the Christian attitude toward life: as there is one Christ, one baptism, one faith, there is one basic morality for all Christians, whether "Jew or Greek, slave or free, male or female" (Gal. 3:28; cf. Col. 3:11) and I would add, gay or straight. Sex is no exception to the inclusive foundation of the moral life—unselfish love for the God and Father of all, and for our neighbor as ourselves (cf. Mt. 22:34–40).

Gays themselves frequently insist that despite a difference in sexual preference, they are just like everyone else—a premise ably supported by a good deal of psychological research. But this is also a *moral* premise; as moral agents, gay Christians must experience sexuality in harmony with rather than in contrast to the rest of common Christian beliefs about life, whether in respect to the spheres of social relations, work, spirituality, politics or play.

Several gay correspondents were very definite about the integrity of Christian moral life, and almost all have flatly (if sometimes regretfully) rejected anything like a double standard for gays and straights. "I think homosexual loving experiences are different from straight loving experiences, especially those in marriage; but love and the obligation to loved one and obligations to all people, are still part of the same unerse in which there are certain moral absolutes." One woman in her early thirties wrote: "I don't see how our moral responsibilities could be different. Maybe I just don't understand what you mean. (I do think it's harder to fulfill our moral obligations—on that I could write a book.)" Another stated, "Yes, I have the same moral responsibilities as my non-gay friends; I do think, though, that morality may have to be specially interpreted for gays—it's scary because there are few 'Christian' models. The only morality that I have considered is that I must respect other persons as children of God; I must not use them for selfish ends; and must allow them to grow—even as I, too, want to grow."

SEXUAL ETHICS

Gay morality concerns sexual responsibility in the over-all context of personal Christian maturity. At root, a sociological as well as psychological matter, moral considerations have definite practical implications. Few if any reliable guides to ethical conduct now exist for gays.[4] But the fundamental healthiness and moral excellence of many mature gay men and women will be manifest in their actual behavior. In turn, that behavior will show, especially over the long haul, certain patterns which are consistent and recognizable as a kind of implicitly rule-governed attitude. There is a pragmatic principle at work here which is found in almost all classical ethics: discover what is ethically appropriate, discover what is characteristic of the decisions, behavior and values of a truly good person.

People are generally aware of someone in their midst who "has it together" and thus functions as an ethical model, probably rather unobtrusively and unself-consciously. In all likelihood, several men and women will emerge as a kind of "corporate model" of maturity and wisdom. Even more likely, these people will not be those who strive to be imitated

[4] A growing ethical awareness can be found, however, in many sources, including McNeill, ibid., pp. 129–48; the works listed in the postlude by Pittenger, Oberholzer, Weltge; and popular works such as on Clark's *Loving Someone Gay*, Millbrae, California: Celestial Arts, 77.

or who enjoy telling others what to do. For an ethically mature person is characterized if by anything a wide-ranging tolerance of other people's behavior and a refusal to become upset or judgmental when others fail to live up to standards he or she spontaneously sets for him- or herself.

As the lives of more healthy and creative gay men and women are examined in literature and film, ethical values and conduct will also become more apparent through the inevitable process of comparison and contrast. Novels such as *The Front Runner, Maurice, Rubyfruit Jungle;* biographies and autobiographies of persons such as Gertrude Stein, Tennessee Williams, Christopher Isherwood, Charles Laughton, John Reid's *The Best Little Boy in the World,* Howard Brown's *Familiar Faces, Hidden Lives;* and films the caliber of *Word Is Out* and *A Special Day*—all have contributed to an emergent sense of gay values capable of undergirding an authentic ethic. Needless to say, many of these stories and accounts will conflict, as values and interpretations often do. But a sincere effort to learn from such vicarious experience will help clarify one's own real values. Every good work of art is a challenge to grow.

Concretely, the fundamental issue of both moral and psychological gay maturity concerns the spiritual quality of a person's attitude toward others with respect to dignity, freedom and ultimate integrity. Christian sexual responsibility then, is the capacity and desire to respond to another person as a uniquely valuable and therefore infinitely lovable Self in terms of bodily intimacy, psychological mutuality and spiritual growth. Such responsibility could well be summed up in two words: reciprocal care. Something less may be far from an exercise in depravity or even sinfulness, but it is nevertheless below the level of what every human person deserves and desires: the best. At the opposite end of the scale is the one-sided, egoistic, other-denying gratification of physical and psychological urges which is aptly summed up as rape. Each human being is aiming at one or other of these goals in every exercise of sexual freedom—toward the fullness of life or toward the vacant anonymity of death. The ethical and religious challenge is, of course, to choose life. Whether we in fact do or not will often be revealed only in the consequences of our behavior. "You will know them by their fruit" (Matt. 7:20).

OBJECTIFICATION

The tendency of many gays to define themselves and others in primarily sexual-genital terms (a tendency strongly reinforced by the gay world) should not be divorced from the same tendency on the part of many straight persons nor from the fact that churchmen have reinforced that tendency in general by overemphasizing sexuality, and primarily negatively. The gay version, however, is doubly disadvantageous. First, gays want to be accepted as ordinary people, not sexual deviants; but a life largely or wholly centered on sex *is* a deviation if sex is only a part of life, however beautiful, important and fundamental. Secondly, such a fixation is severely restrictive. It overrates qualities associated with sexual attractiveness, such as youth, good looks, physique, clothes and "style" to the detriment of equally or more important values such as basic honesty, depth of personality, integrity, spiritual maturity and other life-interests in general.

To be just, it should be stressed that much of the obvious sexual-fetishism of gay life is more a feature of social interaction and recreation—the visible part of the gay ghetto—than a personality trait of individuals. Most gays are invisible at work, school and church—in fact, most are accepted as straight by their non-gay associates. It is in the gay ghetto that the invisibility is replaced by a heightened visibility, heightened in great measure as a reaction against the 9 to 5 masquerade. Nevertheless, it is the after-dark world, where gays can be gay, that the frenetic mating rituals too often identified with homosexuality become a dominant thematic.

Sex is the motif of the ghetto—an inescapable, pervasive, almost demonic presence-to-mind that overshadows or at least fades every other aspect of experience. From a psychological viewpoint, such a situation is rightly called obsessive. In extreme cases, sexual obsession is a serious problem—whether for an individual or a society. In milder forms it seems to be common enough to have left its mark on a considerable portion of American culture. But whether or not we take it for granted, none of us is comfortable with the sexualization of life, nor is the gay ghetto. . . .

The virtually total sexualization of gay life affects individuals variously, but the major effect is one of "objectification" or depersonalization—the centering of attention on genital experience and even the genitals. The psychic fragmentation of personality involved in sexualizing experience produces both psychological and moral disintegration.

The first stage of sexual disintegration is the tendency to relate to oneself or others primarily as sex-objects, even psychically isolating parts of the body from the whole. Interests, values, ideas, conversation, friends and eventually the whole range of experience are progressively narrowed to the sexual element. Acceding to this in the name of an alleged "gay identity" merely masks the actual situation behind a myth. The effects of such objectification have already been mentioned: a never-ending series of affairs, the prolonging of adolescence into middle age, a horror of aging, and few if any lasting relationships, especially on the sexual plane: "in the ghetto, best friends don't screw."

A second phase of personal objectification is the progressive separation of love and sex. It is a mistake to *identify* love with sex, for many forms of love do not involve overt sexuality. Yet to divorce sex from love is to deprive both of their completion. From a Christian perspective, sex without love is a travesty of human dignity; a marriage without love may still be a legal contract, but (*pace* Pope Paul) it can hardly be called sacramental. And in the gay world, sex is plentiful, but lasting love often seems to be forever just beyond reach for many.[5]

---

[5] One strong religious objection to gay relationships is based on the fundamental and traditional belief in the inseparability of sex and procreation, which also provides the basis for opposition to artificial contraception. A deliberate decision to exclude the possibility of procreation is thus considered not only to be gravely sinful, but even to be an invalidating factor if antecedent. However, marriages of sterile couples or those beyond child-bearing age are valid. Further, not every sexual encounter must be, nor is in fact, open to actual conception, thus allowing for "natural" means of contraception, such as the "rhythm" method. The "finality" of the sexual act thus refers *morally* to the in

Such are some of the problem areas of gay sexual morality; positively, the growth-producing qualities and effects of mature gay sexuality are morally equivalent to those of straight sexuality. If I have neglected specifics, it is because I believe, too, that there can be no radical difference between gay and straight morality, despite differences in experience. Values and "disvalues" will be common to both for the most part— for instance, generosity, constancy, fidelity, respect, and responsibility on one hand, and selfishness, promiscuity, betrayal, manipulation and immaturity on the other.

In the next chapter, I shall turn to some particular aspects of gay life in a religious context. Here, I think it appropriate to conclude by recalling the emergence of the church institutionally within the gay ghetto, a harbinger, perhaps a catalyst, of a coming reconciliation between the "Church Catholic" and one of its largest estranged constituencies.

THE CHURCH IN THE GHETTO

The men and women gathered to study and implement the new rite of reconciliation described earlier were members of a local chapter of Dignity, an international Catholic organization of gays and concerned straights founded in 1968 in California. Dignity is committed to advancing the acceptance of gays in the church by promoting worship, spiritual development, education and constructive social action and recreation. There are over 3000 registered members in fifty or more chapters in the United States with affiliates in Canada, Australia, England and Sweden. More thousands of men and women are associated with Dignity-sponsored activities such as liturgies and workshops. Over 800 priests and religious

---

tention of the agent more than it does to the "purpose of the operation."

A gay couple may in fact have no positive desire to exclude procreation from their love-making and may even regret its absence. (For a poignant development of this theme, see Patricia Nell Warren's novel, *The Front Runner* [New York: Bantam Books, 1975, pp. 210ff].) Many gays have even expressed a willingness to adopt foster children. Thus, I suggest, a gay couple could stand in an analogous relationship morally to a sterile or aged heterosexual couple for whom conception is a physiological impossibility but not psychologically or morally undesirable.

men and women are involved in Dignity's work, some as chaplains, others as regular members. A lay movement rather than an official church organization, Dignity has nevertheless been quietly welcomed in some dioceses, while merely tolerated or even banned in others.

Never intended to be a separatist movement, Dignity provides an opportunity for fellowship and worship for Christian men and women who have been rejected by or simply feel unwelcome among their straight brothers and sisters. As a ministry to the "unwanted," it has brought back hundreds to the church and enhanced the religious commitment of additional thousands. The following testimony of a man of fifty is not unlike that of many other gays, most of whom prefer to remain Catholic rather than break away: "I returned to the Church after a long absence through my association with Dignity. I felt the Church was giving me an opportunity to serve God through her as the person I really am." Another commented, "I can hardly conceive of being accepted in a straight parish, unless the world changes drastically. I think gay people will always be, to a great extent, outsiders, and they will find their most meaningful and rewarding experiences in communities like ours." A young woman added, "The beautiful part about *this* gay community is that it is a *real* community. There is a bond, a connectedness, a relatedness, a group feeling, a personal feeling."

Similar organizations or movements for acceptance exist within other Christian and Jewish denominations. The Metropolitan Community Church was founded by Rev. Troy Perry (also in 1968) as a distinct congregation. Protestant and evangelical, MCC has churches throughout the world and claims over 20,000 members. Integrity, an Episcopal outreach program, works primarily within the main body of the church rather than sponsoring separate worship services. Like Dignity, Integrity sponsors national conventions which feature well-known speakers and draw hundreds of participants. Smaller but highly effective gay caucuses exist in Lutheran, Presbyterian and Methodist denominations. The United Churches of Christ have initiated programs, as have the Society of Friends and even some pentecostal churches. Several

Jewish congregations which include admitted gays exist in larger metropolitan areas.

Finally, despite the (fallacious) opinion that, as one venerable religious writer recently informed gays, "You are barred from the priesthood . . . and . . . must be weeded out by religious orders," a rather conservative estimate of the number of homosexual men and women in the Catholic priesthood and religious life, according to a consensus of priests and religious I surveyed at a recent workshop, falls around thirty percent. There seems to be a proportionate number in the Protestant ministry and the rabbinate as well. But I am sure that the percentage of gays in the Kingdom of Heaven will be much higher than that.

Chapter Seven
GAY SPIRITUALITY

As the gay constituency of the Christian community becomes more visible, the need to articulate at least the foundations of an explicitly gay spirituality also becomes more manifest. To many gay Christians, this may seem redundant. For they may well have satisfactorily integrated their sexuality into their Christian life. For other Christians, a gay spirituality represents an impossibility, either because homosexuality is considered an intrinsic disorder, something to be cured or at least to conceal, or, conversely, because it is considered an area of life (like sexuality in general) divorced from spiritual concern.

However, segregating sexuality from spirituality either by suppression or by fission is injurious both to the individual whose life is thus fragmented and to the church itself, which is impoverished by being forced to ignore an important aspect of human experience. If a gay spirituality is possible, it is necessary.

Further, a gay spirituality cannot be redundant, for explicitly or implicitly "straight" spiritualities fail gay men and women precisely where the difference becomes crucial. Despite large areas of mutual concern and actual congruence, gay and straight experience are simply not identical. (Nor for that matter are male and female experience.) To the extent that gay experience is distinctive, a gay spirituality is warranted.

Implicit in the word "gay" is a fundamental affirmation of the positive meaning and moral value of homosexuality as an integral part of personality structure, its functioning and the human condition itself. To be a gay Christian means to expe-

rience being gay as an expression of God's loving plan for
yourself and as part of the human family as a whole. This is
to say that homosexuality has been taken up by the redemptive power of God's Word, who in the person of Jesus Christ
assumed the concrete fullness of human nature—in its fall-
enness as well as its fundamental goodness, else the saving
passion and glorification of Christ would not possess a truly
universal efficacy.

It is more accurate to speak of Christians having a gay
identity than of gay men and women having a Christian identity, but in either case, sexuality represents a partial but integrated factor within the whole personality. Moreover, to the
extent that gay sensibilities, attitudes, values, life-style and behavior find expression within Christian life as a whole, there
the foundations of a gay spirituality are already present.

SPIRITUALITY: CONCEPT AND CONTENT

"Spirituality" is a double-barreled word. Taken as the explicit organization of the religious values and principles by
which persons guide their lives, spirituality has a particular,
even unique, dimension. In this respect, it is appropriate to
refer to spiritualities rather than to spirituality. However,
human life is also always social, religious life included. Even
individual spiritualities are to a large extent derived from
community experience and ultimately from the whole church
as the sacrament of humanity. Thus, every spirituality has an
intrinsic social dimension.

TOWARD A CONTEMPORARY SPIRITUALITY: INTEGRATION

Basically, *spirituality* refers to the fundamental openness of
human nature itself to transcendent experience, that is, the
encounter with other selves which takes us "out" of ourselves.
Spirituality thus also refers to the actualization of the capacity
for transcendence by actual encounters of many kinds, involving some dimension of trans-subjective reality which is
raised to conscious awareness, organized and cultivated as a
way of life. This "method" or way of life will always have an
intrinsic social dimension; all spiritualities derive from and
feed into the ongoing experience of society and civilization as
a whole.

More concretely, spirituality will deal with the constitutive elements of individual and social experience: the "I" or Self, including the dimensions of body, mind and spirit; the World of natural and social objects, "He," "She," "They" and "It," with their various relations; the Other Self, irreducible to the objective world, "Thou"; and, ultimately, the ground of all these, their encompassing field of reference which is the most fundamental condition for the possibility of any experience. It is the function of religion to reveal this "ground of experience" as God, the "Thou" of the World.[1]

Christian spirituality is not so much a science as an art, the art of living. It respects and cultivates the bodily aspects of experience, including the sexual dimension. Mental discipline or meditation enjoys prominence. Specifically spiritual aspects of life such as the appreciation of beauty and the desire for goodness, the quest for justice, reverence for life, humor, playfulness and especially friendship all find place. Further, spirituality as a process will be organized according to priorities which each person assigns to the values represented by these characteristics. It will be expressed poetically and in action rather than speculatively. For symbols and myth, like gestures, convey what concepts and measurements cannot even comprehend.

Thus, by spirituality I mean an individualized style of living in which body, mind and spirit are consciously integrated in terms of a freely chosen system of values centered on God's self-communication through the experiences of self, nature and society and expressed in the form of worship and service.

Christian spirituality will be *God-centered,* finding him present in scripture, sacramental celebration and in the world itself as the medium of his creative love. And thus it will be *prayerful,* a direct response to God as Thou in praise, thanksgiving and petition. But it will also be social, actively expressed in the work of justice, peace and friendship in the world. It will, likewise, be *natural,* rooted in a fundamental

---

[1] I am here indebted to the thought of William Ernest Hocking, the rudiments of whose philosophy of spirit can be found in *The Meaning of God and Human Experience,* New Haven: Yale University Press, 1963.

awareness of God's active presence in creation. It will be no less *historical*—grounded temporally in the saving events by which God fashioned himself a people. It will to that extent also be *ecclesial*, an awareness of the commonality of salvation realized here and now in the institutional and spontaneous aspects of the church's corporate life. Above all, it will be *Christological*, finding in Jesus Christ both model and mediator between God and human persons, "the human face of God," to borrow Hocking's phrase.

Spirituality is above all else an integrative art, or, more accurately, a *re*-integrative one. We begin life as infants—well-integrated but hardly even conscious and certainly unable to function independently. We mature and slowly gain control of our powers, but by dint of the world's brokenness, we arrive at self-conscious maturity more or less dis-integrated physically, psychologically and spiritually. We often need healing before we can develop further. Thus, there is a *therapeutic* aspect to spirituality. Re-integration remedies our deficiencies and guides us along the way to fuller health—bodily, mental and social. Spirituality guides this integrating process by providing a model and a method, both organically related to a coherent set of values.

The model and the goal of the process is the *whole* person, ultimately Christ himself, the full Christ—head and members. The work or method of spirituality may be largely implicit in the social transactions between the person and the community, integration progressing more or less unconsciously. But this work may be facilitated and even abbreviated (or, better, condensed) by making it consciously explicit.

The dialectic of integration, dis-integration and re-integration has been given various designations through the centuries. In Christian antiquity it was called, simply, the mystical life, later "the three ages" of the interior or spiritual life—the purgative, illuminative and unitive "ways." While positive in their orientation, these stages were, in later centuries, interspersed between "negative" transitional stages, the "dark nights" of the senses and the soul, here following St. John of the Cross. A modern writer, Dr. John Lilly, refers to the process as one from "orthonoia" through "paranoia" to "metanoia."[2]

Importantly, there are social factors at work in all three stages of the spiritual dialectic. Part of the negative process which a human being has to undergo in order to become fully healthy includes the identification of and detachment from the socially conditioned values, concepts, attitudes and behavioral patterns which every child uncritically because unconsciously adopts in the course of socialization itself. These social factors are not only a mixture of helpful and hurtful elements, they are powerfully compelling, the more so to the extent that they continue to function unconsciously.

In fact, if a person did not spontaneously come to the often painful recognition of the social construction of reality and the need for disengagement in order to become morally and conceptually autonomous or "self-actualizing," it would be necessary for spiritual maturity to induce such a detachment. For only when a person has acquired at least a minimal degree of social independence can she or he freely choose to adopt from among the goals, values, ideas, attitudes and patterns of behavior available in a society which can constitute a personally meaningful life-style. Thus, all detachment is for the sake of re-attachment.[3]

The process of social deconditioning may occur spontaneously but without the supportive structures of an explicit spirituality to provide both the framework and control by which the process can be systematically advanced. Detachment occurs prematurely or without awareness of the possibility of re-attachment, disintegration without the hope of re-integration. A serious fragmentation of personality may result. Thus, many schizophrenics are probably undeveloped or aborted mystics, just as many tramps, thieves and other social misfits could be considered arrested saints.[4] This bears impor-

[2] See *The Center of the Cyclone,* New York: Bantam Books, 1973, and *The Programming and Metaprogramming of the Human Biocomputer,* New York: Julian Press, 1972.

[3] Cf. Arthur C. Deikman, "Deautomatization and the Mystic Experience," *Psychiatry,* Vol. 29 (1966), pp. 324–38.

[4] Cf. Kenneth Wapnick, "Mysticism and Schizophrenia," *Journal of Transpersonal Psychology,* Vol. 1, No. 2 (Fall 1969), pp. 49–66, and Roland Fischer, "A Cartography of Ecstatic and Meditative States," *Science,* Vol. 174, No. 4012 (26 November 1971), pp. 897–904.

tantly on the situation of gay persons who have uncovered the
mechanics of social determinism and the limits of social conditioning. To that extent they are free of them, but may have
no alternative integrating framework and control system to
turn to except that of the gay world itself. Perhaps the only
genuine alternative to becoming "paranoid" or a creature of
the ghetto is to develop an explicit and authentic spirituality.

The social basis of spirituality, its anchorage in the deepest
values and highest aspirations of the human species, provides
through the concrete experience of men and women every-
where and at all times a relatively transcultural structure
which can undergird the program of social disengagement,
thus establishing a fundamental continuity of experience. It
also provides criteria of evaluation and a range of options out
of which a personal value system can be constructed. Further, it supplies the concrete opportunity and resources for
the process of controlled withdrawal from and return to society to take place. This it does by functioning as a way of life
in a supportive community funded by years, perhaps centuries
of collective experience, supplying motivation in the form of
encouragement and goals, and providing guidance or direction by skilled helpers. If the group embodying these elements
concretely has a history of any scope, there will also be concrete models or examples to imitate or surpass in the form of
heroes or saints. This will be as true of the gay world as of
any cultural system.

The culmination of the dialectic of spiritual development
occurs when a more or less continuous stage of personal
unification is retained, although the persistent brokenness
of the world guarantees only approximate success in this
achievement. Further, unification is not attained by primarily
attending to one's own progress, but by a progressively closer
identification with the transpersonal Other. Full spiritual development can only be realized in social experience, because
we are social beings by nature. The Unitive Way is thus
marked by an ever-growing awareness of oneness with God
and also of oneness with our brothers and sisters "in the
Lord." This unity is first and primarily realized in the mutual
dialogue and self-giving of true worship. It is secondarily but
equivalently found in the re-entry into the world of the other

ou's, nature and society, wherein the God of mystical
awareness also works and waits. The sign of true sanctity
(which literally means wholeness or integrity) is *charity,*
agapē, a love which is expressed tirelessly in service and care.
But connected with this divine love is an equally powerful
thirst for justice and the spread of justice in all human rela-
onships. The mystic, for so we may name the one who has
begun the quest for the ultimate integrity of human life, is
so the prophet.

But the achievement, or rather, the inauguration of final in-
grity is not the simple effect of a human process of spiritual
evelopment. It comes at last as a gift for which we can only
make ourselves ready by ridding our lives of obstacles and
positively surrendering our efforts to reach God. The communication of God in love to a heart made receptive by aban-
oning its own plans for fulfillment is called *grace*—the freely
ven and shared life of God himself.

TOWARD A GAY SPIRITUALITY

In light of this sketch of the foundations of Christian spirit-
ality, a gay spirituality will be distinguished by reference to
e specific characteristics of gay experience constitutive of a
ealthy identity and life-style, both individual and social. First
f all it will be *gay.* The transcendent dimension of experi-
nce must be found in context of the life-situations of gay
ersons. Likewise, the integration of body, mind and spirit
ill involve the situation, difficulties, opportunities and hopes
f gay men and women. The social aspects of worship,
iendship and justice will also reflect the exigencies of gay
e and society as well as relations with straight men and
omen and facets of social prospects and oppression.

Spirituality is a social process. For all of us, the very ele-
ents of spirituality are derived from others—and in particu-
r from our immediate environment with its specific atti-
des, values and patterns of behavior. That is to say, most
irualities are somewhat uncritically fashioned from the
oup spirituality, whether deeply religious, highly secular or
blend of both. But to undertake the spiritual life earnestly
quires raising the tacit spirituality we have inherited to

fuller awareness, subjecting it to critical evaluation and refash
ioning it to fit our individual needs and aspirations. Thus
individuality itself is a function of the social process and
through it every authentic spirituality becomes at least a cri
tique of society.

A gay spirituality, too, will reflect the social structure and
dynamics of the gay world as a social subsystem. It, too, wil
require raising to greater consciousness the positive and nega
tive factors latent in gay experience, assessing them in orde
to incorporate what is constructive for each individual an
the community. An authentic gay spirituality will thus als
function as a critique of the gay world within the context o
the wider social milieu.

Of particular importance here is the "deautomatizing"
power in being gay, which endows the gay man or woma
with the ability to see with different eyes, that is, to disengag
themselves from the value-systems uncritically accepted in so
ciety at large. This can be frightening and even dis-integra
tive. It can also be liberating, both for gays and ultimately fo
straight people. Specifically, it gives gays the power to risk de
cisions about life which straight men and women because o
their greater stake in the dominant social system cannot eve
consider.

SOCIAL DIMENSIONS OF SPIRITUALITY

Although the vast majority of gay men and women ar
"out" only in a very limited sense, an authentic gay spiritu
ality must recognize that acceptance, association and actio
represent the cutting edge of a fundamentally healthy ga
identity, individually and collectively. In a society rendere
increasingly homogeneous and colorless by mass commu
nication, transportation, commerce, education and ente
tainment, being a member of a subculture possesses distinc
advantages for anyone seeking a meaningful niche in the soci
world. For a gay man or woman, a sense of commonality, c
having a special character which, although not freely choser
nevertheless relates them to other gays throughout the worl
and offers a distinctive place and role. It isn't a wholly con
fortable niche—but it does serve to differentiate them fro

e mass society, if somewhat negatively. This subcultural
entification process should not be underestimated as a fac-
r in a person's decision to come out—or, rather, to *stay* out.
can have an inhibiting effect on personality development if
mere compensation for failing to achieve a more ordinary
cial identity. But it can also open up possibilities for growth
d personality development, apart from any question of sex-
l indulgence. In either case, the social experience of gay
en and women bears on spirituality as an encompassing way
life.

The more or less traditional opinion of spiritual writers that
mosexual men and women should avoid all situations, per-
ns or references connected with homosexuality—in other
ords, to stay in or go *back* into the "closet"—has become
tenable today. For by encouraging suppression and denial
the case of an inclination as primal and powerful as sexual-
, such advice will probably produce not mental peace but
eater distress, anxiety and explosive episodes of compul-
e sexual indulgence. "Being out" is by far a more positive
ute with regard to mental health, and true mental health
d spirituality will not be opposed.

Flight from the gay world is no more "spiritual" than flight
m the world in general. On the other hand, uncritically
entifying yourself with the whole gamut of experiences, in-
tutions and life-styles in the gay world is just as much a ca-
ulation of moral discernment and autonomy as is the sad
d mindless conformity still too characteristic of our life in
ciety. It is even more foolish to place yourself in a situation
which a real moral failure is practically inevitable. The
age of Socrates and St. Bernard is still effective: "Know
urself" . . . and act accordingly.

In short, spiritually healthy gay Christians of the future
ll more likely than not be known—selectively—to be gay,
d most will certainly not masquerade as straight. This will
as true for sisters, priests and brothers as it is for layper-
ns. For a gay man or woman to be called to a life of dedi-
tion to God in the service of his people does not differ from
e vocation of straight men and women. In some respects,
wever, such a life for a gay person will be more difficult,
t because of temptations, but because of the extreme "ho-

mophobia" found in seminaries, convents, novitiates and th institutional church as such.

The process of "coming out" itself has many of the chara teristics of religious conversion, as noted earlier. With regar to personality integration, it can have the same function in gay spirituality. But in this respect, as in the other, entrustin yourself to God by saying "yes" is not the climax. It is on the prologue. The exuberance wears off, and the let-down i either case can be severe as the convert begins for perhaps th first time to face the responsibilities and day-to-day grind follow-through. It is at this point that a realistic and workab spirituality is most necessary.

TRANSCENDENCE

Gay spirituality as a radical capacity for transcendent exp rience is essentially no different from that of anyone els However, societal pressures on gays are generally greater ar their awareness of the need for a deeper source of person security and worth does, I think, affect their readiness to de with the transcendent dimension of human experience in positive way.

The great depth-psychologist Carl Jung expressed this we years ago when writing about male homosexuality in "Th Mother-Son Complex." (I believe his remarks pertain less to Lesbians.) "Often he is endowed with a wealth religious feelings, which help him bring the *ecclesia spiritua* into reality, and a spiritual receptivity which makes him sponsive to revelation."[5]

Whatever Jung meant by the *ecclesia spiritualis*, it is ev dent that many gay men and women are remarkably sensiti to religion—both positively and negatively. Few gays I ha met are indifferent about it or the church, especially concer ing the role that the latter has played in oppression ar discrimination—and still does. On a deeper level, gays a perhaps acutely aware as a minority group of the prete tiousness and brokenness of the social world. This, I thin

---

[5] C. G. Jung, *The Collected Works*, trans. by R. F. C. Hull, N York: Pantheon, 1959, Vol. 9, p. 87. I am indebted to Fr. John M Neill, S.J., for bringing this passage to my attention.

also accounts for their evident openness to signals of trancendence from beyond the wreckage.

Here, too, I find a clue to the almost characteristic "fixing" enthusiasm which is virtually a gay stereotype. With what I can describe only as a kind of yearning for grace and beauty, gays seem to have a penchant for rehabilitating old houses, preserving architecture, restoring antiques, conserving park areas, playgrounds and old traditions of all kinds. Whole sections of urban blight have been renovated largely by the effort and example of gays. Similarly, many gays can be found in the healing and service professions—doctors, dentists, nurses, paramedical personnel, orderlies, social workers, therapists, counselors, clergymen and lay ministers, teachers and more. It is as if both the human and aesthetic wreckage of society appeal in a special way to the sensitivities of those who have also suffered rejection—and who thus richly fulfill Henri Nouwen's description of the "wounded healer."

Gays are also susceptible to sentimentalism and aestheticism, just as they are to insensitivity and even vandalism. Given the bright side, the shadow should be expected to have the same contour. But overall and for a variety of reasons, the capacity for transcendence, that is, for ecstatic experience, seems well-developed among most gays. A hint of this appears even in anthropological and archaeological studies of religion, especially of shamanism. Eliade and other researchers point out that among many pristine cultures, homosexuality was taken to be a sign of divine election.[6]

BODY, MIND AND SPIRIT

The corporal aspects of spirituality have always lurked in the background of classical treatments, but generally the body was treated as an enemy to be purged, mortified, punished and generally scorned. This persistent Manichaeism still injects a large part of contemporary spirituality, but the tide is at last turning.

The body is far more than a container for the soul. It is the

[6] Cf. Mircea Eliade, *Shamanism*, New York: Pantheon, 1964. For an overview of such evidence, see Karlen, op. cit., pp. 464–65 and 39–40.

soul, the Self, made manifest—the visible sacrament of the human spirit. Our treatment of the body, correspondingly, is a metaphor or an index of our attitude toward ourselves. Today especially, when a negative self-image seems to be the native endowment of the race, it is vitally important to begin a spiritual program therapeutically—by "unlearning" abuse of the body and learning how to befriend and "tune" it properly.

This is true in general in our society. But because of the traditionally severe and negative attitude of society and the church toward homosexuality, it is even more urgent for gay spirituality to reintegrate the self corporally. Negatively this means neither pampering yourself, substituting cosmetic art for true care, nor abusing yourself physically or permitting yourself to be abused. Positively, all the dimensions of bodily personality need to be understood, appreciated and cultivated. This entails not only developing some effective body-consciousness, but attending to the "asceticism" of proper diet, exercise, rest, eye care, skin and hair care, dental hygiene and the maintenance of the various internal systems —including the bodily aspects of sexuality.

To abuse, neglect or permit abuse of the body is symptomatic of psychological and spiritual problems. Caring for yourself, conversely, touches on some sensitive areas of our society in general—alcohol consumption, other drug use—including the "ordinary" drugs such as caffeine, nicotine and the various barbiturates and other ingredients of sleeping pills, pep pills, etc., and, of course, smoking. More exotic forms of chemical ecstasy are common in the gay world. But the body can tolerate only a limited amount of physical abuse, no matter how "enjoyable," before lasting damage results—including damage to the mind and, proportionately, to the human spirit. Acquainting yourself beforehand with the effects even of mild drugs such as marijuana and "amyl" and especially the more dangerous kinds—amphetamines, cocaine, opium and heroin—can prevent serious problems later on.

[7] Cf. *Man's Body* by the Diagram Group, New York: Bantam Books, 1977, pp. H-1 to 52, and for a discussion of drug use among gays Mark Freedman and Harvey Mayes, *Loving Man*, New York: Har. Publishing Co., pp. 115–20.

Affirmative action with respect to the physical dimension of
ur existence is the bedrock of any contemporary spirituality.
egular exercise and periodic medical checkups are no less
eneficial to gays than to straight people and with regard to
nereal diseases, more so. Similarly, weight-watching, body-
uilding and dance, like more ordinary athletics, can be excel-
nt forms of ascetical discipline.[8]

SPIRITUALITY AS MINDFULNESS

The Greek ideal of a healthy mind in a healthy body has
t been superseded by the industrial revolution and the
omic age. Because of them, in fact, we are probably less
cely than our Attic ancestors to preserve either physical or
ental health despite our spectacular triumphs over certain
seases. "Getting your head together" pretty well sums up
e challenge, both for gay and straight people. But in many
spects, the passage from orthonoia to paranoia is shorter for
ys, given the hostile emotional climate in which they are
rced to live. The clear message to every gay man and Les-
an at one time or another, even all the time, is simply that
ou are definitely not OK." But the journey to metanoia,
ight-mindedness," is far from impossible for gays even in
e midst of continual accusations of mental or moral pathol-
y. In many ways, considering the enormous pressure con-
antly weighing down on them, gays may even be healthier
an their straight counterparts.[9]

With regard to gay spirituality, mental integrity consists in
ght thinking and right attitudes about yourself, the world at
rge and those special thou's in the world. As a condition for
ental freedom, disengagement from the ordinary social
ocess of conceptualization may come easier for gays, as

[8] Among recent publications in this area, see *Man's Body* and
oman's Body by the Diagram Group; Gay Luce, *Body Time,* New
rk: Bantam Books, 1973, and Frances Lappé, *Diet for a Small
anet,* New York: Ballantine Books, 1975. An excellent theological
dy is John A. T. Robinson's *The Body: A Study in Pauline Theol-
y,* London: SCM Press, 1952.
[9] Cf. Freedman, "Far from Illness: Homosexuals May Be Healthier
an Straights," *op. cit.*

noted before. However, disciplined thinking, like thinking fo
yourself, is no one's patrimony. Merely substituting one set o
social concepts for another is no solution to the problem o
mental dis-integration. A person has to relearn how to thir
by first unlearning some bad thinking.

In spirituality, the art of thinking has traditionally bee
called *meditation*. Fundamentally, it is the ability to arre
conceptual thinking and to cultivate awareness—experiencir
the simple fact of Be-ing. As a mental discipline, meditatic
recreates the mind as exercise and rest refresh the body.
simplifies consciousness by expanding it and thus helps r
store psychological integrity. From a religious perspective, tl
art of meditation in its many varieties has but one goal: t
rid the mind-field of distracting images and concepts and th
to "tune" it to the pervading presence of God, the uno'
jectifiable Ground of all our experience. As the volunta:
stillness of meditative concentration gives way to an effortle
contemplative "gaze," still a deeper form of non-analyti
pre-reflexive awareness, the human spirit has completed t
preparation and must await the free gift of God's presenc
now not as the Ground of Experience dimly perceived, but
our Friend and Companion.[10]

As noted before, from the viewpoint of a gay spiritualit
perhaps the most salient feature in the process of meditatic
is its power of breaking down habitual modes of thinkin
that is, of "deautomatization" or dishabituation. Havir
shaken loose the pervasive control which socially determine
concepts exercise over thought by suppressing conceptu
thinking itself, it becomes possible to develop independe
habits of thought by simply reflecting on what, or who, yc
truly are. No one is ever absolutely free from the constrain
of social patterns of knowledge and value, however; huma
freedom is always relative. But breaking loose from absolu

[10] On meditation, see William Johnston, S.J., *Silent Music*, No
York: Harper & Row, 1976; Lawrence LeShan, *How to Meditate*, No
York: Bantam Books, 1974; Claudio Naranjo and Robert Ornstein, *T
Psychology of Meditation*, New York: Viking, 1971; Thomas Merto
Contemplative Prayer, Garden City, N.Y.: Doubleday Image Boo
1971, and *Contemplation in a World of Action*, Garden City, N.Y
Doubleday Image Books, 1973.

dependence on the social matrix is nevertheless real freedom, if relative—and no less dizzying for that.

Once spirituality is understood as the attempt consciously to integrate the various components of experience into a lifestyle centered on certain fundamental and freely chosen values, it is not difficult to see that sexual identification and social roles must play an important part in spiritual development. Ignoring or repressing them not only fragments the spiritual life, but permits sexuality to dominate it unconsciously. By contrast, a healthy spirituality will incorporate masculinity and femininity, generativity and support. Further, sexuality will be recognized as an essential interpersonal dimension of life, not a matter of private preoccupation.

For the gay man or woman, positively integrating sexual identity and role, including the aspect of orientation or emotional preference, presents particular challenges and opportunities. From a social perspective, to begin with, socially conditioned models of identity and role are discovered not only to be in most respects inapplicable, but also to be highly relative. Even the stereotypes of masculinity and femininity more or less unconsciously imported into gay life-styles as "butch and nelly," "dyke and femme" characteristics served mainly to point out the artificiality of such enforced poses. Today, the resistance of many gays unwilling to be so superficially categorized has led to a greater exercise of creativity and responsibility in constructing styles of life satisfying to individuals on their own terms. Conversely, by sharply separating maleness and femaleness from cultural conceptions of masculinity and femininity, gay life-styles and *even* poses have had a liberating effect on straight society itself. Pure femininity is as much of a chimera as is male superiority, white supremacy or Western civilization.

In terms of spirituality, integrating various competencies and exploring interesting role possibilities become a program of self-liberation and personal development. Similarly, resisting the force of social systems bent on imposing roles on supposedly malleable individuals becomes a necessary, if negative, preliminary in developing a positive spirituality.

SPIRIT AND VALUE

The realm of spirit concerns aspects of experience which are not easily analyzed—truth, freedom, happiness, beauty reverence, humor, peace and the awareness of supreme worth, goodness and right. Above all, I would include here the intellectual love of God, human friendship and the sense of wonder.

Basically, spirituality concerns *values*—what we esteem in things, persons, events and life itself. But not in the abstract or as static. Rather, spiritual values are always concrete, alive and above all, active. Any spirituality which does not lead to active involvement in human affairs is unchristian.

Here, two fundamental kinds of value will serve to exemplify the rest—justice and friendship, which—with worship—virtually encompass what is worthwhile in experience Thus, as we near the conclusion of this sketch, we return to our original theme.

WORSHIPING

Worship represents the explicit acknowledgment of God in which the human spirit replies "Thou" to the divine self-communication in all the graced moments of life. As a moment in a dialogue, worship has an aspect of responsibility about which suggests a form of justice. For worship recognizes and ratifies the right relationship, the *bond* between creatures and their Creator. Worship is also a form of friendship, for it also binds human persons together in corporate forms of prayerful celebration. Like human justice, our active expressions of praise, gratitude, reparation and petition are moved from within by love. Worship is the vertical dimension of loving service in the human world.

In the gay part of that world, worship is not a manifestly predominant factor—but a movement toward God is nevertheless clearly present in the love of life and quest for meaning there as well as the hunger for right relationships. Further, well-attended religious services sponsored by the Metropolitan Community Church, Dignity, Integrity and other Protestant, Orthodox and Jewish groups testify to the vitality of that religious sensitivity Jung had recognized so many years ago. In fact, the national and international networks of such religious organizations represent the largest gay organizations in the world.

JUSTICING

Gerard Manley Hopkins' "The just man justices" (from *Kingfishers Catch Fire*) grasps the essential meaning of the thing. Justice is an active effort to bring about right relationships in every area of life, to inaugurate the Kingdom of Heaven. The heart of justice is compassion—the ability to care for others, in particular those who suffer. Among gay men and women, who have certainly tasted the gall of political, economic and religious oppression, compassion should come easily and justicing follow as a matter of course.

Today, few countries still prosecute gays for private, consensual behavior between adults, the United States being one of the few, but discrimination continues. It is thus not surprising that much of the justicing of the gay community concerns gay liberation. But gays cannot afford to limit their concern to themselves. For all minority groups are necessarily linked in a common struggle for *human* rights—not gay rights, black rights, women's rights, Indian rights, Chicano rights or old people's rights, but the fundamental rights of *all* people.

Active solidarity among gay men and women and other minorities is the kind of political expression of faith that a contemporary spirituality must enhance.[11] Minimally, it calls for active participation in the ordinary political process and the fulfillment of civic responsibilities, guided by a radical love of freedom and human dignity.

THE SPIRIT OF FRIENDSHIP

Jung again was keenly aware of the spiritual potential of homosexuality concerning affection, (non-erotic) friendship

[11] For a further discussion of the political implications of spirituality, see *The Mystical and Political Dimensions of the Christian Faith*, Claude Geffre and Gustavo Gutierrez, eds., New York: Herder & Herder, 1974 (*Concilium*, Vol. 96).

among members of the same sex and even between men an
women—so often antagonists in a grim psycho-social war o
the sexes. Homosexuality, he wrote, referring specifically bu
not exclusively to male homosexuality, "gives him a great ca
pacity for friendship, which often creates ties of astonishin
tenderness between men, and may even rescue friendship be
tween the sexes from its limbo of the impossible."[12]

The greatest and for that reason the most challenging d
mension of human life is the achievement and developmer
of true friendships. Love in its wide sense is not only th
deepest and most universal of all human values, it is in lovin
that we discover most directly in our experience what *Go*
means. Human loves are the sacrament of our love for and b
God. Friendship as inclusive love, "unconditional positiv
regard," is the nucleus of all spirituality, condensing all as
pects of corporality, consciousness and social concern int
one act of integration. Love is not only our most radical ca
pacity for transcendence, it becomes real only as actual reach
ing out and joining with Others, beyond oneself and yo
within oneself, that is One Self: "You in me and I in you
(John 14:20).

Love is ultimately One but not one-dimensional. It is th
Poet's "many-splendored thing." C. S. Lewis wrote of th
"four loves"—sexual love, affection, friendship and charity.
These are four *ways* of loving, each a manifestation of a d
mension of human life. For gay men and women, as for ev
eryone else, spirituality integrates the various loves of ou
lives, developing the art of loving appropriately to the situa
tion in which we and our loved ones discover each other. No
all loves will be erotic, not all affectionate or amicable. A
can, however, be expressions of charity—*agapē*—which bin
all the others together.

So integrated, all our loves will be *transcendent*—an escar
from the prison of self-centeredness, a going-out-of-ourselve
to Others and therefore *ek-static*. Secondly, our loves w
be *inclusive*—not actually including everyone in particula

[12] Loc. cit., p. 86. For an insightful commentary on this passage, c
John McNeill, S.J., *The Church and the Homosexual*, pp. 137ff.
[13] C. S. Lewis, *The Four Loves*, New York: Harcourt, Brace, Jovan
vich, 1960.

which only God could encompass in the sweep of his infinite solicitude—but extended to everyone we meet. Again, the ways of loving will vary—erotic love will probably be the most restrictive, because of its very intensity. Affection and friendship (*philia*) will extend outward much farther. But *agapē* does in effect open us to all creation—it is non-exclusive love, God's love loving through us. It is a general, universal love, particularized by each actual encounter, but only as restricted in the long haul as is our experience.

With regard to gay love, what is important to note here is that it will extend outward inclusively, from the intimacy of *eros* to the openness of *agapē*. And while *eros* may well be limited to those of the same sex, the other loves are not, and must not be cut short by "heterophobia." The most pressing danger to gay men and women who do not associate with the opposite sex except by necessity is that the feeling, even the attitude, that the "other" sex is superfluous may become a reality.

The complementarity of the sexes is not primarily a matter of physiology. Psychologically and socially, having real friends of the opposite sex(es) is *necessary* to activate the bisexual personality components in every man and woman, which is to say, for true sexual integration. Suppressing one or another aspect of sexuality distorts our personality, our experience of life. It produces psychological and social imbalance. That bias is both reflected in and engineered by the exclusion of "the others" from one's circle of friends, whether because of fear, hostility or plain indifference.

For gay men and women (and for straight people as well), it is therefore spiritually necessary to have not only gay friends of both sexes, but straight friends of both sexes as well. The Lesbian who can't relate to straight women is no more healthy and integrated than a straight woman who can't relate to Lesbians. The same holds true equally for men. The relative proportions of male and female, gay and straight friends will vary for every person; the main issue is that each of us needs to know the rest of us, and by knowing, learn to love.

Chapter Eight
RESISTANCE

All Christian spirituality has a dual aspect, a positive and a negative side. For while fundamentally optimistic about the radical goodness of the world and especially of its human inhabitants (Gen. 1:1–31), Christians have never long deceived themselves about the "brokenness" of that world, including the tendency in all of us toward sin—both individually and collectively. Christianity takes evil seriously, but not too seriously.

Much of the preliminary phases of Christian spirituality as the art of integral living has a negative tone, then, because it recognizes the necessity of confronting the real evil in us and around us. More accurately, there are *therapeutic* aspects of spirituality which concentrate on healing the wounds of sin and overcoming the brokenness of the world. To that extent, spirituality *can* be re-integrative, poised against the forces of disintegration from within and without. But the main thrust of Christian spirituality remains positive and, as such, developmental. It aims at fostering growth, once destructive agencies have been identified and the process of resistance begun.

As Christian, gay spirituality, too, will have its negative aspect—one of resistance, protest and reform which concerns the destructive forces of the gay world perhaps even more than those stemming from the fear, ignorance and prejudice of straight society. But also as Christian, even a minimally adequate gay spirituality will possess a more fundamental and positive emphasis on growth toward the full humanness of a mature and creative faith.

For most gays, at least those convinced that they, too, are

God's friends, the challenges they face both from the straight world and from their own world can be summed up as a diminishment of self-worth, the relentless if not always overt prejudice and discrimination they meet in daily life, a lack of meaning—both being misunderstood and the failure to grasp the meaning of their lives—and, finally, the manipulation and exploitation based on their orientation.

The miracle of gay life is not that there are not failures and tragedies, for there are, but that there is so much love, laughter and health in the gay world, to paraphrase Evelyn Hooker. The courage and resilience of gays is not just the embattled defiance of a besieged minority group, but a strength that derives from profound human resources and subtle perceptiveness "well-seasoned with wit." (Col. 4:6) From a spiritual viewpoint, gay men and women live in a situation in which they must constantly reaffirm the meaning and value of life or be thrown back into confusion, hopelessness and estrangement. One of the greatest values gays offer to society in a broken world is the sense of human value itself.

Evil exists in the gay world as well as around it; resisting sin and evil thus warrants consideration here. The positive elements of Christian spirituality provide a response to personal sinfulness as well as to sinful social structures.

SIN AND EVIL IN THE GAY WORLD

When Dr. Martin Hoffman subtitled his study of male homosexuality "the social creation of evil," he touched on the nerve which, from a religious viewpoint, is possibly the most sensitive of all. Few groups in modern society are so encapsulated by morally destructive social forces as the gay community. In large measure, the very existence of a gay world is a product of social evil: fear, ignorance and persecution from straight society and exploitation and degradation arising from within the ghetto. Gays' successes in resisting these truly demonic powers by living according to positive ethical norms, as well as by Christian moral values in many cases, testify to a persistent spiritual strength. It also points to what I think is the major work of Christian gays—the redemption of the gay world itself, by authentic witness and by creating alternatives to the morally destructive forces and structures of that world.

The distinctive Christian awareness of sin is not only realistic but healthy, because human evil is a real dimension of every person's experience apart from all questions of determinism; it can be overcome. Sin in this sense means the failure to realize ultimate values in everyday actions, as well as manifest violations of moral norms. As responsible persons we all have to acknowledge as honestly as we can the sins we commit or condone, but we have an equal, even prior responsibility to know when we are *not* sinning.

One of the major blindnesses of moralists in considering homosexuality (and sexuality in general) has been the failure to see that the central problem of sin and evil is not the "rectitude" of individual, physical acts, but the structural forces of the societal systems in which men and women must live. These contextual elements, truly evil social structures, must be considered as at least precipitating factors in the moral struggle of gays.

Further, real sin and guilt must be discerned in terms of the fundamental attitude of the individual person toward other persons, toward himself or herself and toward God—the totality of life's values and meanings. The "essence" of sin in the personal sphere is the elevation of *myself* to an all-important status, so that everyone, or, more accurately, *some*one is reduced to the status of an object for my desire or use without regard to his or her dignity, needs, desires or well-being. Sin is not just selfishness, but also "otherlessness." Ultimately, it is the failure to love, whether by refusal or by violation.

Thus, the sexual "sins" of teenagers (in particular) and many adults should not be seen so much as disordered acts or the experience of forbidden pleasure as the failure to treat themselves and others with the care and love they deserve.

Several individual problem areas have already been considered in previous chapters, and there is little need here for more than a summary. Basically, moral difficulties fall into three groups:

1) *Personal diminishment:* "ontological guilt"—the belief that gay is bad and that, therefore, gays are evil. Insecurity, dependency, passiveness. Escapism—fantasy and isolationism. Materialism.

2) *Sexual irresponsibility:* Self-indulgence, infidelity, an obsessive preoccupation with genital sexuality, sadomasochism.

3) *Interpersonal falseness:* "games," evasiveness, affectation, stereotyped behavior, deception, dishonesty.

There are also particular temptations of members of any sub-group, especially an oppressed minority. First: to deify its virtues and excuse its faults. *Idealization* is a fancier name for it—the process by which the underdog triumphs over its adversaries by wishful thinking. The attempt to live up to a merely ideal image can be comical—or grotesque. The *macho* male, an image so prevalent among young Latinos, is a caricature of masculinity. But when acted out, it produces vicious results: the degradation of women, the brutalization of men, artificiality, games, the perpetuation of a destructive sexual mythology. "Homosexualism" is no less a caricature than *machismo*—it is also no less destructive and degrading.

Second: the plunge into *ideology,* a natural aftermath of a dip into idealization. It represents a falsification of thinking to justify a destructive or inauthentic life-style—a kind of rationalization. Allowing patterns of behavior to influence thought patterns to the extent of losing the capacity for individual decision-making and independent action is humanly injurious to anyone. This is one reason why we all need to be able to "unwind," and just "be ourselves." Otherwise, social roles tend to become permanent identities, and it is here that gay life can be a trap. Escaping the enforced masquerade of the daytime business world into the nocturnal gay world can be a mere shift from one set of artificialities into another.

Labeling represents a form of ideological strategy which has few if any beneficial aspects. Being typed, especially as a social deviant, and whether by oneself or others, carries with it not only a degree of stigmatization, but action-expectancies. A labeled person is expected to behave in a certain fashion, which is taken to be emblematic of the whole class. Usually, the behavior comes about one way or another by the curious dynamics of the "self-fulfilling prophecy"—Once a thief, always a thief. Labeling further permits society (i.e., other people) to deal with "deviants" (i.e., trouble-makers, dissidents) in short order: most simply, by dismissing them as "bums," "queers," "hippies," "commies" or what-have-you.

Thus, before accepting or adopting the label "homosexual," it is advisable to consider carefully the kind of expectations, limitations and attitudes that are attached to the label. Coming out can be restrictive as well as liberating, both in and out of the ghetto. *Gay* is not merely a verbal tag to which people are indifferent.

It also seems to me that straight people (not just heterosexual persons, but non-deviants in general) will tolerate a good deal of so-called deviance in others so long as the "different" social behavior, including sexual matters, is kept private, that is, devoid of public attention, banners, placards, slogans and . . . labels. Avoiding being labeled, importantly, is vastly different from either staying in the closet or "passing" as straight. Basically, it means (again) being yourself. If *that* isn't acceptable, labeling won't help.

Conversely, the straight world's resistance to labeling is highly selective and can be a forceful way of preventing constructive confrontation. As long as blacks could be called Negroes, black pride and black power could be kept at bay, psychologically and socially. Similarly, either by keeping gay men and women safely in the closet or by perpetuating formal labels such as *homosexual,* the challenge of gay pride and gay power can be avoided. It is as short a step, further, from homosexual to "queer" as it was from Negro to "nigger."

Thus, coming out can be an equally forceful way of instituting social change by initiating a change in consciousness, first among gays themselves, then among straight people. A person may have valid reasons for not coming out "all the way," but there are equally valid and perhaps more urgent reasons for strategic public acknowledgment. But no one should be forced to come out, whether by straight pressure or by that of gay militancy.

SOCIAL SIN

It is temptingly easy to harp on the social immorality of the gay world as it is to rant about the alleged depravity of individuals. But it would be equally foolish to ignore the immense problems presented to gays by their partially created, partially inherited environment—a moral climate which, for good or ill, cannot be completely avoided even by gays who have little to do with the ghetto and its subcultural excrescences—films, magazines, hardware, etc.

Many of these have already been mentioned, others need little comment: the rejection and abandonment of gays by gays, the depreciation of the aged, ugly and "ungifted," the epidemic of venereal diseases. Fundamentally, the sinful social forces of the gay world themselves fall into two major classes: immoral environmental institutions and exploitation.

The negative impact of the bars, baths and films, as well as cruising, tricking, etc., has been traced before. Most of these environmental factors can be summed up under one rubric: pornography.

THE SEX TRIP: PORN

Pornography is not merely vicarious "sex thrills" packaged in cheap plastic, but a mentality that is both pervasive and subtle. It is the belief that human sexuality and thus human persons are cheap, vile and marketable.

Perhaps the most insidious enemy gays face is porn: the deep, secret fear that despite all the liberal rhetoric sex is not only dirty, but evil. It is not so much said as lived. Sexual contact among homosexual males (especially) is too often reserved for anonymous encounters, whether in public washrooms, steam baths, casual pick-ups in parks and on beaches, one-night stands following a chance and terminal meeting at a gay bar or theater. Such furtive, often commercial and hastily forgotten experiences are *not* just the result of straight oppression, for they perdure in areas where consensual sexual activities in private are not illegal.

Much of the message of gay magazines and newspapers,

films and cockbooks, as well as the environment of the bars
and baths only reinforces a pornographic conception of sex
—not, of course, that it is evil and sinful, ideas alien to
gay culture and media ("church porn"), but that sex—or,
rather, orgasm—is a constant and undeniable need and therefore a right which must be satisfied as frequently and easily as
possible.

Any human activity voluntarily pursued under conditions
of anonymity, haste, darkness, the fear of being caught or
even seen can hardly indicate psychological or moral health.
To the extent that an intolerant and repressive society has
contributed to these conditions, the society itself is pornographic, and those caught up in it are more pitiable than
worthy of prosecution. But the overall situation cannot be ac-
counted for in terms of reaction. And to attempt to glorify
or justify the situation is far more pathological than merely
being victimized by it.

"SEXPLOITATION"

In every restricted social group, there will be people both
eager to be of service and those ready to exploit that limited
sphere for everything they can get from it. It should not be
surprising that along with gay counseling services, legal aid
programs, VD clinics, benevolent associations and religious
missions there are also brothels, bars, baths, bookstores and
other establishments that range from mildly parasitic to vam-
pirical. Many of these institutions exploit gays by promoting
activities that not only pay well but encourage compulsive behavior.

It should be recognized, however, that few if any of even
the most dehumanizing institutions in the gay ghetto do not
have counterparts in the straight world. Nevertheless, what
makes the situation more oppressive and tragic in the ghetto
is that the intermural exploitation of an already socially
oppressed minority is being engineered by gays who are only
too willing to make a dollar out of the skins of their brethren.

Not all "recreational" establishments that cater to gays are
equally or even deliberately exploitative, and some have positive aspects. Most, however, seem obviously prone to adver-

tise in terms of the lowest common denominator in the gay world: the promise of easy sex. A good many of the "crotch ads" in gay papers are half-parody, but the impression remains that the main appeal is genital. The ads are by no means misleading in many instances.

Specific forms of resistance against personal diminishment, sexual irresponsibility and interpersonal falseness can be as simply enumerated as were their opposites: honest self-evaluation and acceptance; discipline, restraint and altruism; fidelity and constancy; realism about oneself and the gay scene as well as the straight world; empathy and compassion for straights as well as gays; openness, simplicity, truthfulness; commitment to growth.

Social challenges require action as well as character: legal reform and education, protest against intramural exploitation, the creation of alternatives for meeting and recreation.

Against the power of pornography stands not a puritanical "Aunt Nancy" mentality which swoons at the mention of sex and which is thus no less pornographic, but rather a truly humane and Christian attitude toward sexuality. The authentic Christian vision is based solidly on the conviction, laboriously achieved through centuries of experience, that sex is neither shameful nor sinful, but morally excellent and spiritually ennobling, a gift and thus a grace which in its true human enjoyment brings men and women into the creative mystery of God's life and love.

Similarly, in regard to sexual exploitation, it is one thing to disapprove of the baths, beaches and bushes for oneself, but what of others? Keeping *your* head together in a bar with a bad reputation counts for little if your presence there constitutes a tacit recommendation for others. Moreover, your patronization contributes financially to the further exploitation of your gay brothers and sisters.

Even creating alternatives to the dehumanizing sexual circuses of the baths and other concrete forms of exploitation will accomplish little if the existence of such establishments continues without any kind of resistance or criticism. Not long ago on the east coast, a gay bar notorious for its exploitative activities was successfully picketed by militant gay liberation forces. Such liberation can be achieved, and should be, by gays themselves, who can afford to be no more tolerant of gay exploitation and the "soft" oppression it represents than they are of straight persecution.

MORAL GROWTH AND THE
DISCIPLINE OF LOVE

Traditional Christian references to the qualities of moral strength and behavior have been so abused and disemboweled by pettiness and Jansenistic body-phobias that the very words "virtue," "chastity," "purity" and "modesty" evoke mainly comic sentiments or anger.

"Chastity" means nothing other than the responsible and creative expression of our God-given sexual capacities for mutual fulfillment—physically, psychologically and spiritually. Christian sexuality involves, as a consequence, fidelity, sensitivity to the needs, moods and abilities of the other, mutual generosity, respect and integrity. Such a contextual understanding of sexuality also implies a foundation of permanent commitment, constancy and trust.

Discipline and restraint have been traditionally (and wisely) indicated as necessary conditions for the responsible expression of sexuality, especially in terms of genital relations. Known to the ancient world as *modestia* or "moderateness," such active control is called for in several important areas of life, even those lacking an immediate connection with genital behavior. In a brilliant phenomenological analysis of sexual behavior, St. Thomas Aquinas pointed out four: recreation, dress, self-esteem and curiosity (cf. his *Summa Theologiae,* II-II, QQ. 160–161, 166–169).

Moderation in recreation means acquiring the kind of self-control over our gestures and behavior which most people identify with good manners. Thomas insists that play and recreation are necessary for a balanced life—jokes, light conversation and games are mainly what he had in mind—including athletics. *Modestia* here becomes for Thomas friendliness or affability—the avoidance of injury, sarcasm, obscenity and excess.

In a Christian perspective, this recalls Paul's suggestion to the Colossians (3:8f): "You must give up being angry, bad-tempered, spiteful, using abusive language and dirty talk; and never tell each other lies." (Cf. also Phil. 4:8 and Eph. 5:3–5.) The touchstone here with respect to sexuality is a preoccupation with genital behavior as a topic of conversation and jokes. In the gay world, the immediate context is camp, gossip and sexist language.

While generally innocuous, camp can easily become destructive when directed against someone in a malicious way or even if intended as good-natured "dishing" it exceeds the intention and causes embarrassment, humiliation or offense. Camp can also substitute for open and intimate conversation, becoming a verbal game that is both evasive and manipulative, whether by merely keeping conversation on a trivial level of puns and innuendo or by tightly controlling the direction and depth of the dialogue. Another problem camp provides through its double-entendres and oblique comments is the strict, if not sharp, focus on sex, which further strengthens the preoccupation with mating details tying much of gay society together verbally.

The close connection and sense of solidarity in the gay world permit a good deal of talk about what (or whom) people are doing—probably the most common topic of any gay conversation. The combination of a highly effective grapevine with an insatiable interest in everyone's affairs produces a tough brand of gossip. Accounts of affairs, break-ups and breakdowns very easily cross over from "newsflash" to detraction and calumny. But besides the loss of reputation implicit in the dynamics of gossip, there are other problems: the betrayal of confidences, trust and secrets—without which intimacy and friendship can hardly exist. Gossip also functions as a leveling mechanism, quickly whittling down anyone who has "pretensions."

A final talk-trap associated with camp is the use (mainly if not exclusively, by males) of cross-gender references. While it may be superficially just "crampy" to refer, for instance, to a man as "she," such inversions are indicative of deeper attitudes, specifically a sexist bias. For the feminine pronouns and nicknames are used basically *as* camp—for comic effect, mild irony and sometimes vicious verbal abuse. But never in anything but a condescending manner. Authentic liberation in the gay world demands the eradication of such degrading patronization of both women and men.

REGALIA

Thomas next discusses moderation in dress—a particularly important area in the lives of most gays, especially those who enjoy the bar scene and the late night parades in the ghetto. Cruising has much to do with dress of course, and, in addition to clothing itself, keys, handkerchiefs, chains and almost anything which can be worn can be used to indicate availability and preference. Modesty in clothing is thus not merely a matter of not arousing people by accentuating the sexual organs, buttocks and breasts, but also concerns an excessive interest in clothing for reasons of vanity and ostentation as well as a studied *lack* of care about clothing which can be just as effective a way of attracting attention. Beyond leading someone on, a preoccupation with clothes, jewelry, cosmetics and hairstyles, the proper shade of tan and the right pose can too easily replace care for the deeper elements of personality, as mentioned before.

In this, a compensating concern with appearance, typical of many gays and lesbians as well, is hardly worth caviling over. But there is the likelihood that things will not end in mere compensation, which *is* worth a word.

The body should be cultivated, celebrated and adorned as the house of the Spirit as well as the manifest, personal "you." But moderation here is as necessary for balance, both mental and spiritual, as it is in architecture and design. Attempting to excite someone sexually by dress, as well as by conversation or behavior, is merely solicitation; doing it for "kicks" is adolescent and irresponsible.

SELF-ESTIMATION AND
RESPECT FOR OTHERS

Thomas' main concern with *modestia* is not merely with clothes and raunchy behavior. The kinds of moderation he especially emphasizes are proper self-esteem and intellectual simplicity—what the medievals called humility and studiosity. *Humilitas* means having a modest opinion of yourself—that is, a true estimate of your own worth, without the embroidery of pretense, exaggerated self-regard *or* self-depreciation.

Whatever "studiosity" brings to mind today, Thomas' fourth kind of *modestia* counters the tendency toward unbridled curiosity, which is not a mere eagerness to know, but a desire to know too much. The insatiable desire to know it all, especially about people, leads to snooping, prying and considerable wasted energy, tending as well toward gossip.

An ethic of moderation in behavior, dress, self-reference and people-interests may, indeed *will*, appear to many as a quaint and puritanical hold-over from some sexually repressive period of history. The mordant observations of Aquinas and his sources indicate just the contrary; they knew what they were talking about and their remarks still, almost curiously, strike home. (Aristotle: "It is a mark of effeminacy to let one's cloak trail on the ground to avoid the trouble of lifting it up.")

From a psychological point of view, one not absent from Thomas' thinking, the restraint implied in *modestia* has an important function in a cultural situation in which the glorification of sex has reached heights as idolatrous as any in past ages. Restraint means being self-possessed, liberated from the competitive tyranny of the sexual meat-market. Avoidance of some places and persons will probably be necessary for many in order to retain the basic self-respect which should characterize an integrated person. But from a Christian point of view, the ability to conduct oneself responsibly in an irresponsible situation rather than retreating from it has the added value of witness and example. Not the pharisaical self-righteousness which can simply substitute for other forms of sexual gamesmanship, but the lived testimony of a balanced, playful but inner-directed person. A real Christian presence is redemptive, but not obtrusive; it should convey a sense of freedom to those around, not one of inhibition.

Paul certainly had something like this in mind when he encouraged the Christians of Philippi "to act in everything you do without grumbling or argument; prove yourselves innocent and straightforward, children of God beyond reproach in the

midst of a twisted and depraved generation—among whom you
shine like the stars in the sky" (Phil. 2:14–15). He con-
cludes, "Let your *modestia* be evident to everyone" (4:5).
To the Colossians he wrote, similarly, "Conduct yourselves
intelligently with those who are not Christians, and make the
best use of your time. Keep your conversation pleasant and
flavored with wit [literally, 'salty'] so that you will know best
how to respond to each person" (4:5–6).

THE FORGOTTEN OPTION

The ordinary opinion of moral theologians in the past was
that among possible life-ways open to homosexual men and
women, celibacy—the state of dedicated singleness, that is,
total abstinence from any active sex-life—was the only acceptable choice. Recently, theological voices have raised the
possibility of a responsible expression of sexuality for those
outside the married state in special circumstances: widows,
single men and women, and gays. Recognized moralists have
also countenanced permanent homosexual relationships as a
"lesser evil" than a life of promiscuity for gays when celibacy
is not a live option.

While I am not sure that "lesser evil" is an appropriate designation for a faithful, constant and loving human relationship, I wish here to suggest that celibacy, too, should be
given thoughtful consideration as an authentic and fully responsible life-style for gays insofar as it represents a free decision.

As a Christian life-style, celibacy must be freely chosen for
the sake of the Kingdom of Heaven as a response to a call
from God recognized by the church either publicly or privately. It would be an abuse of language to call the irresponsible bachelorhood of the straight or gay "swinger" celibacy, even though it may well be a freely chosen state.
Likewise to call celibate the enforced state of criminals, the
required state of military cadets or the involuntary condition
of being unmarried would be confusing and wrong-headed.

Celibacy as a responsible expression of sexuality is not fundamentally a mere "discipline" in the Roman Catholic
Church; it is a spiritual, indeed *mystical* identification with

Christ, who, as the coming Lord, transcends the structures of
this world, including marriage. (Married love also has an
"eschatological" character, however, in the unselfish commitment of husband and wife, who embody in their mutual love
God's love for his people in Christ—see Eph. 5:21–33.)
Without the manifest relation of the freely accepted renunci-
ation of marriage and genital sexuality for the sake of the
Kingdom, the single state has no specific Christian value as
such, and if involuntary, represents an unfortunate human situation.

"Celibacy" as the enforced state of singleness many churchmen woud require of homosexual Christians as a necessary consequence of their sexual orientation is anything but
a free response to a grace of God. It is more punitive than the
forced deprivation of convicts, who are sometimes allowed to
marry even while imprisoned. Such a demand differs radically
from both the celibacy of priests and religious as well as those
lay persons who take private vows, for it takes no account of
either the desire of the person or his or her ability to live
celibately—a situation unthinkable for candidates for the
priesthood, the religious life or for those who live celibately
in the world. (In fact, the alleged *inability* of gays to ob-
serve celibacy is one reason adduced for refusing them en-
trance to the priesthood and religious life!)

The practice of forced celibacy is clearly at odds with traditional Christian theology. The alternative, of course, is to
recognize as valid for gay Christians a way of life, if not tan-
tamount to marriage, at least open to some form of sexual expression. This the church has been unwilling to do, and thus
arises the dilemma of the Christian, gay *or* straight, for whom
neither celibacy nor marriage are psychologically, personally
or spiritually desirable or even possible.

Celibacy should remain a real option for Christian gays,
however, whether in the priesthood, the religious life or as a
consecrated life-style in the world. Homosexuality cannot *require* grace, which is essentially a free gift; it can, however,
be an occasion for grace. And despite seminary rectors, nov-
ice mistresses, pessimistic bishops and diocesan columnists, it
is quite evident that many homosexual priests and religious
are serving God's people faithfully and responsibly throughout the world.

IN SPIRIT AND TRUTH

The most urgent matter at issue which gays need to address is neither theological nor political, but spiritual. A shift in political positions or theological understanding without a corresponding advancement in spirituality would be shallow. Moreover, as a cohesive and motivating force, a spiritual breakthrough should accelerate the process of theological and political liberation, and it would also provide reserves of strength when setbacks occur. Furthermore, the church as a whole is undergoing a crisis of spirituality, in no small part due to the irresistible fragmentation produced by the confrontation between Christianity and the modern world. More than ever in an increasingly interdependent world society there is a need today for diverse Christian spiritualities applicable to particular situations and groups.

A gay spirituality will be rooted primarily in the gospel of Jesus Christ; that is, it must be radically Christian, more indebted to faith in Christ than reliant on spiritualities of the past few centuries. A vital spirituality always develops in the encounter between the Spirit of Christ and the emergence of a new situation or group in the church. Gays are such a group today, despite the fact that there have always been homosexual Christians, because our understanding of homosexuality has changed more radically in the last twenty years than in the previous twenty centuries.

Spirituality is not just applied theology—if anything, theology is probably distilled spirituality, the experience of Christians alive to the meaning of their existence. Spirituality always involves actual experience. Hence the spiritual theologian has to be especially sensitive to the lessons of the whole Christian experience, just as individual Christians should be attentive to the achievements of their predecessors. However, their primary resource will always be the New Testament. They will also be guided by the collective experience of the church embodied in its teachings, but they will be alert as well to new needs created by changed situations.

Gay Christians, too, must appropriate the spiritual inheritance of the whole Christian people, especially as recorded in the lives of its saints and mystics. There are, however, no autobiographies of gay saints—at least none we know of. *As* gay saints, today's men and women must write their own spiritual autobiographies, aided by mutual sharing and reflection. Their stories may some day be a source of inspiration and guidance for other gay Christians as the writings of Augustine, Teresa of Avila and Dag Hammarskjold have been for countless persons.

While the emergence of an authentic gay spirituality is not yet in sight, several elements can be suggested. I believe, first, that Jesus and his mother will occupy central roles as models of faith—Jesus, the loyal witness and now the Transcendent Lover, and Mary as the woman of faith, the faithful hearer—and doer—of the Word. God will be seen not merely as Father, but as the patient lover, the God of Hosea and John the Evangelist. The Holy Spirit, *the* Advocate, the Spirit of love, prophecy and peace, will be sought to guide further experiences of unity and acceptance. Finally, the church will be discovered more to be a filial association, brothers and sisters united as adult citizens of God's kingdom, rather than an organizational hierarchy of clerics imposing burdens on the masses without raising a finger to help lift them.

Spiritually, the experience of gay Christians constitutes a virtual model of radical faith according to the mind of Paul and reaffirmed by Luther; we are saved solely by God's grace through faith. There is nothing we *can* do to merit salvation, nor to justify ourselves, thus nothing we *need* do.

Here the existential element surfaces and leads us to the mystical and prophetic dimension of gay life. To the sometimes awful and painful cry, "Why me?" there comes a reply, not so much in words as in an experience of free acceptance by God. As one young gay wrote to me: "When I started attending Mass again after my separation from the church, I prayed to Christ while looking at the large crucifix above the altar. The prayer was simple: 'Are you for real and there for me?' During Holy Week services a couple of years ago, I got my answer. I said my little prayer as always but this time Jesus looked down at me and said: 'Yes, I am real and I know about your being gay, but I don't care. My love is for you, too.' I went home and cried."

Chapter Nine
THE JOY OF BEING GAY

Sunday, June 27. Gay Pride Week is drawing to a close with the annual parade and rally. Hundreds of gays and lesbians are· already marching as I arrive—as usual, fifteen minutes late. Some are on floats, some astride cars, a few on roller skates and skate boards. Thousands of spectators line both sides of Broadway. There is little heckling and no violence. Many gays exchange campy wisecracks and banter with the spectators. As I glance over the crowd it makes sense— perhaps a third of the people on the street are wearing gay pride buttons or other identifying tags.

Banners, tee-shirts and chants herald the various groups: "Gay and Proud," "Gay Power," "Gay and American," "Two, four, six, eight—we don't overpopulate!"

"Hello, padre," smiles a Puerto Rican woman as I pass on the sidewalk, outdistancing the parade. I smile back, wondering if I should say something.

A large black banner is carried by. The group is from the Institute of Human Relations, a gay service center. The banner describes the pink triangle Hitler forced homosexual prisoners to wear in the concentration camps before slaughtering a quarter million of them. Pink triangles on black armbands are visible here and there throughout the crowd. . . .

A black man in his early twenties stops me: "Hey, man— do you believe this?" "It's a fact," I answer, struggling for a reply: "You don't believe in facts, you accept them." "I've seen this thing for three years and I *still* don't believe it!" he laughs and walks on. A huge cloth snake slithers by, green with a black head and lots of human feet. Its legend: "Don't tread on us!" Nearby wiggles a Chinese dragon, someone thrusting a popsicle into its toothy mouth, toward a much smaller mouth—human and parched.

The parade will strike me later as an almost perfect model of the gay world. There are representatives from every element of the ghetto—female impersonators on cars and floats, some professional entertainers, others obviously amateurs. A couple of baths have elegant floats, as do the more successful bars—one of them a leather-and-chains pub which caters to the *macho* S & M crowd. The men on the float are all in leather, one strapped to a wooden frame. "Love takes many forms," says a sign.

Somewhere else a banner reads, "Ladies, do you know where your husbands are camping tonight?"

Various associations are represented: Mattachine—named for a clown; One, Inc.; several gay newspapers from Chicago, Milwaukee and South Bend; and service organizations—Gay Horizons, the Gay Peoples Union, the Human Relations Institute, the Rainbow School for the Deaf, its riders striped with every color conceivable. . . .

The church is there: MCC has a large delegation with liturgical banners, cars and a float. Several marchers are wearing clerical collars; they see me, smile and wave. Dignity has a big birthday cake atop one of its cars—a bicentennial theme. One of the chaplains is marching in black suit and collar. Alongside him, a young man who broke his foot three days ago is hobbling along on crutches, sweat streaming down his face. It's over ninety degrees. Several marchers see me and wave—a few shout. For a while, I walk with them. It feels odd, uncomfortable at first—but I begin to feel a sense of pride and admiration, as well as an unusual awareness of something else—meaning, point, the scope of it all. I'm not sure what.

After a few minutes, I rejoin the spectators to see the rest of the parade. Integrity is coming up toward the end—a small but brave showing. Once more, a priest is walking with his people, a tall, dignified man, no doubt suffering from the heat, but easily keeping pace with the younger men around him. I wave, but he doesn't see me—his eyes fixed steadily ahead.

Almost at the end of the parade, I see something that I hadn't expected, and my throat constricts—clowns. Over six of them. In full, gaudy costume, their faces painted with huge smiles. They're releasing balloons and chattering with the crowd. . . .

Somewhere a marcher with a black child on his shoulders shouts, "Children are beautiful, too. . . ."

At the beginning of this essay, I claimed, perhaps whimsically, that clowns provided a clue to the meaning of being gay. Unpacking that clue is not so much a theological or psychological exercise, but a venture into something more like poetry. It involves a certain view of life, one almost peculiarly Christian: the comic vision. I will try to explain.

Earlier, I also said that the gay world is a microcosm of the straight world, a kind of model, accentuating both its positive and negative characteristics. As such, the gay world can provide a valuable contribution to the larger society—reflecting its image back, with commentary. Socially, the gay world has a critical capacity which is all too frequently wasted; that of being a magnifying mirror held before society, particularly with respect to its most often uncritical attitude toward sexuality.

In both the critical capacity and its failure, gay men and women share a triple vocation: that of the artist, the mystic and the prophet. The distinct touch of gayness involved focuses this threefold sensitivity to aesthetic value, justice and celebration into the image of society's mime: the clown. It begins with the ability to see what others do not see, and the will to create through suffering.

THE CREATIVE RESPONSE

It is something of a myth that gays—especially men—are "artsy" people: ballet dancers, interior decorators, hair stylists, actors, window dressers, organists, painters, poets, and so on. But, just as many great athletes and jazz musicians are black, so too many great artists in every field are gay—and there is the nucleus of the myth.

Gays have no corner on the arts; most artists are not gay.

But the fact that many gays are highly sensitive to aesthetic values and the likelihood that a somewhat disproportionate number of artists *are* gay raises an important question regarding art and homosexuality.

Part of the answer lies, I think, in the openness of the arts to people who may be "different" in many respects but are gifted with artistic capacity. On the other hand, many gays probably gravitate to the arts because of that openness, even those without great artistic talent, content merely to be accepted, if not to shine. But there is, I think, an even deeper reason: the affinity of the artist and the gay person in terms of a fundamental sensitivity tied to a different outlook on the world, one often sharpened to a critical focus by social rejection and personal suffering.

Artists and gay people are, in relation to "straight" society, misfits and often outcasts, relegated to the fringes of respectability because of the discomfort their vision of reality and its expression produces in their contemporaries. Frequently, artists behave oddly (as the saints themselves do), driven by their muse, genius or daimon. They live intensely, drinking life's joys and pains to the dregs, burning themselves out in the effort to communicate what they have seen to an unreceptive world.

Artists have been called the "antennae of the race," because their heightened sensitivities "pick up" meanings and values which the rest of us miss. The social contributions of artists are inestimable in this regard, even apart from the vast and important service they perform in delighting and awakening us to beauty by reassembling, distilling and merely pointing to the spectacular richness of human experience in the natural and social world.

Gays are, in this sense, artists of sexuality, for they reveal by their presence, their mere *being*, the meaning and value of human sexuality. Heterosexual love as the normative bond between men and women and the foundation of family life is not challenged or inhibited by homosexual love, but distinguished and made more visible. Without homosexuality as a "paranormative" beyond of heterosexuality, much of the significance and worth of heterosexuality would be swallowed up by the everyday, taken-for-granted ordinariness that pervades our lives.

Gay men and women "raise consciousness"—merely being with gays or lesbians comfortable in their own orientation calls straight men and women to question themselves, perhaps not so much consciously as existentially. Men or women uncomfortable with their own sexuality may respond by attacking, just as people uncomfortable with life often strike out at artists. Others are less upset, but few are left indifferent.

But gays do not exist merely to heighten people's appreciation of heterosexuality; they no less jarringly propose that male-female relationships can exist on the basis of mere personal attraction, by choice in friendship (*philia*) rather than *eros*. Such a realization is not only beautiful and valuable in itself, it is also liberating, for it frees us from our fears of same-sex friendships, too. One of the gravest threats to contemporary civilization is the peculiarly western, male fear that *any* close ties with a person of the same sex is deviant, sick or immoral. Here, too, gay love, by the contrast of opposition, provides a way out of the trap: close friendship need *not* be a function of sexual magnetism. The cure for homophobia is homophilia.

PROPHECY

Gay sensitivity to the structures and pressures of society, the capacity created by a constant awareness and experience of difference, passes from the artistic to the prophetic as art itself does when it portrays reality truthfully and thereby challenges us to change. For the truth about life is not only its beauty, but its disfigurement and its possibilities; the aesthetic sense becomes a moral sense when it perceives what can and therefore should be.

Social criticism is thus a major contribution of gay existence—again not by actual intention so much as by unavoidable result. Sexual oppression, injustice, prejudice and discrimination are revealed by the way society treats gays and other despised minorities. All the self-hatred, fear and doubt of a male-dominated world—both civil and ecclesiastical—has been unleashed at some time against those whose love is so threatening to the masculine mystique. Women's liberation and gay liberation are inseparably linked by being the product by protest of unbridled male domination.

The prophetic aspect of gay experience comes to light particularly in protest against injustice, thus revealing a heightened if perhaps narrow sensitivity to justice. (The limited scope of the justice sought is not detrimental to the true prophetic vocation. If anything, it is characteristic of it, for abstract or general justice is merely an idea or at most a disposition. The prophetic crisis usually involves concrete cases with wider implications, witness Amos and John the Baptist, and in our own time, Martin Luther King and Dan Berrigan.)

As the forgotten beauties of love impel the artist to awaken an automatized society to the meaning of sex and friendship, so the suppressed nobility of justice urges the prophet to call our attention to reform. He may do so haltingly and symbolically, like Jeremiah, or with the thunderous eloquence of Savonarola and Calvin, the quiet humility of Gandhi, or the courageous dedication of Dorothy Day and Mother Teresa. The duty of the prophet is to teach—to educate, *e-ducere*—to lead out of darkness into light. And here gay men and women must instruct both the state and the church.

The ways of teaching and re-teaching (reformation) are multiple. Passively, gay men and women can teach both society and the church by permitting bona fide researchers to learn from them the meaning of gay experience. This entails the willingness to share their views, life histories and responses. It also involves work. Both require courage and dedication to the cause of enlightening the darkness too many gays and straights are forced to wander in.

Gays, like other groups explored and sometimes exploited by social scientists, are sometimes understandably reluctant to open up their lives to any form of investigation. Here, the prophetic call of the gay community demands the sacrifice of some personal privacy for the good of all. The more that is learned about the varieties of homosexual experience and the health of gay men and women, the sooner will suppressive myths be destroyed and the policies which flow from them reversed.

Prophecy is a primarily active ministry, however, both in

civil society and the church. Any spirituality which does not eventuate in some form of social action is not authentically Christian. The prophet is called (and often cannot refuse) to criticize, to sensitize, and to protest. The prophet is one who "professes"—who speaks up and speaks out, who will not remain silent in the face of injustice. The prophet is also a transformer, converting words into action.

In the gay community, active prophecy involves the responsible and productive education of the straight world by an energetic attack on myths, stereotypes, oppressive laws, attitudes and acts of discrimination. By *responsible*, I mean in response to the authentic vocation to prophecy—an ability to listen to the voice of God and to discern the signs of the times. I also mean responsiveness to the actual needs of situations in which fallible human beings find themselves. Gay activists cannot afford the diversion offered by lashing back merely in anger or in the hopeless attempt to achieve full liberation overnight, much less to overcome all opposition and misunderstanding. *Productive* prophecy means, accordingly, efforts having realistic goals which in turn effect real changes; it also means the refusal to be misled by merely symbolic victories and rhetorical consolations.

Prophetic effectiveness likewise entails honesty and good faith—virtues whose absence or weakness among the oppressive majority provides even less excuse for overlooking the real problems of the gay world. Gays must address themselves prophetically to the correction of abusive situations in the ghetto, the visible reinforcers of straight fears, myths and hostility. Social acceptance will remain an ever-retreating hope so long as efforts to reform the position of straight society are vitiated by moral cracks in the ghetto.

Gay social activists must be accountable to the gay community as a whole, furthermore, and here the responsibility for assuring accurate representation falls to the ordinary gays and lesbians who are not militant, but whose destiny is no less involved in the struggle for acceptance than their leaders. Similarly, it is vital that the unoutspoken give encouragement and support to their spokesmen and women, whose experiences in city halls and chanceries may be soul-battering. Jesus said,

"Anyone who welcomes a prophet because he is a prophet
will have a prophet's reward" . . . (Mt. 10:41).

MYSTICS AND ARTISTS

Listening for the voice of the storm-God of justice and the
whisper of the loving Father's compassion ties the acute sensitivity of the artist to the aggressive out-speech of the prophet.
Every true prophet is first a mystic—"one who closes his
eyes" (and mouth) in order to hear and feel the presence of
the Friend. And every mystic is an artist—a person of heightened awareness, disciplined in the ways of expressing truth
and beauty.

All human beings are probably mystics and artists in the
beginning; most of us simply have it drilled out of us by age
five or so by the hum-drum of the "everyday." Gay people
are hum-drummed, too, but their constant burden of difference, their felt rejection in the mind and often at the
hands of society prevents them as a group from foreclosing
the aesthetic and mystical realms of personality so effectively,
simply because they can never fully identify with the greater
society. The hum-drummer misses a beat every so often, and
in that still moment, when the "beat of a different drummer"
can be heard, there is a chance for infinite adventure as the
worlds fly apart. Here beauty arises in guises invisible to
most. And here, often in the beauty, sometimes in the pain,
whispers and thunders the voice of the Lord.

It is no less a capitulation to myth to maintain that gay
men and women are more open to God than others—yet,
there is a peculiar religious sensitivity among many gays that
is distinctive and not too easily dismissed as a substitute for
parental love missed in childhood. For the church has not
been a kind mother. . . . Nonetheless, as with the arts, it is
likely, though unproved, that a disproportionate number of
ministers, priests, sisters, brothers, rabbis, sheiks and shamans
are homosexual—disproportionate in so far as the percentage
is slightly higher than in other professions.

But mystical sensitivity is not the same as a vocation to the
ministry and need not be stifled merely because the church so
often slams the seminary door in gay faces, to its own great

loss, I should add. And here arises the need for a gay spirituality that is not identified with a professional "vocation," yet not excluding it.

JUSTICE AND LOVE

Christian spirituality has a twofold foundation in justice and love. The prophetic ministry of justice is not antagonistic to the mystical vocation to love—they complement each other, in fact, require one another. Love, in the Christian ethic, has a kind of primacy, however—and hence it is, I think, that the true prophet is first a mystic, which is to say that real love leads to active "justicing." The love of God which is the beginning, center and culmination of the mystical life is not separate from human love, which is its emblem and often its medium.

Perceiving God's love in our human loves *is* the Christian mystical experience, just as it is constituted in general by a consciousness of God's presence in moments of ordinary experience: anyone can grovel before a burning bush. Revelation is not a parting of the clouds and a majestic voice, but the sense of presence, the communication of a Self in love and support, an invitation to growth and service.

There are three elements to note with regard to the mystical dimension of life, whether gay or straight: the grace of the present, living for the Kingdom, and the universalization of love. In each case, the structure and the discipline of mystical experience is provided by the exigencies of love. For gays, the ways of creating and sustaining responsible love will be, I think, the essential and ultimate achievement of their spiritual lives. For Christian living means loving rightly —integrating sexuality into the whole of life, subduing love's enemies and surviving the tests of love. That is to say, loving responsibly, faithfully and trustingly, despite the unnerving onslaughts of anxiety, jealousy, possessiveness, self-centeredness and romanticism; enduring the tremendous challenges of unreturned love, loneliness and the greatest of all human trials, the loss of love. Such *is* the crucible of the spirit, and in that the vessel of God's presence in this life.

Traditionally, the mystical life has been characterized by

an acute sensitivity to that presence—not in the past experiences of men and women centuries dead, but in the here and now. Discernment of the grace of the present moment is what distinguishes mystics from those who follow more authoritarian routes, which, whether in literal obedience to scripture or the regimen of liturgy, are both safer and more orthodox. For the outcast and oppressed, it is more urgent to grasp what God is doing now and will do in the future than what he has done before, however.

The future, "eschatological" element of mystical life—is especially relevant for gays and lesbians, whose awareness that they have no lasting city here is perhaps more naturally acute than that of straight persons. Gays may be forever tempted to transform the immediacy and transciency of gay life into a permanent sense of being "out of place." But living for a cause which transcends the physical and temporal limits of the world, whether expressed in specifically religious ways or in the quest for lasting meaning and value—for truth, justice and well-being—avoids the traps of materialism, sensualism and surface-existence, and also achieves a continuity surpassing the "ordinary immortality" of procreation and providence.

The eschatological dimension of spiritual life must (and generally is) related to the service of real persons, not general ideas. The great mystics *typically* translate their love into concrete acts of human devotion, often seeking out the most unfortunate and unwanted members of society. In compassion for their own brothers and sisters, as well as other dispossessed people, a compassion heightened by the struggle against rejection and oppression, gays become able to continue the real tradition of mystical work in the world: prophetic action.

SEND IN THE CLOWNS

It is not mere whimsy that now brings me back to the image of the clown, for in it we find, I think, the embodiment of the artistic, prophetic and mystical components of gay experience, touched throughout by an uncanny sense of the truly comic character of human life. Whether in modern versions such as those of Carol Burnett, Jackie Gleason or Marcel Marceau or the ancient figure of Mattachine, the Moorish street-fool with his drum, his dance and his rags, the clown has always signified the will to create through suffering.

Clowns really do not belong in circuses. Like giraffes and elephants, they have been domesticated and rendered innocuous by imprisoning them for entertainment's sake. As our Roman and medieval forebears knew, clowns belong in the halls of government, on city streets and in church councils. They expose human pretensions to divinity and remind the powerful as well as the meek wherein resides our true godliness. But our Calvinistic, Jansenistic moralism with its somber and tragic view of life has banished the jester and the court fool. Only the saints seem to have preserved the great work of the clown—the Fools in Christ who, in the Eastern church, perform extravagances that demolish the sober pieties of the righteous and undo the real vanities of the all-demanding world. And St. Philip Neri, balancing pillows on his head while dancing for children in the streets of Rome. And the *hilaritas* of the early monks which left a now-lost heritage of Feasts of Fools and Asses in the medieval church, ceremonies which began on the Feast of the Holy Innocents and ended with Mardi Gras.

When I see gays as clown figures, I am not attempting to create another stereotype, but to grasp the meaning of a clue as to the deeper significance and worth of homosexuality in civil life and the church. Here, "clown" is no term of contempt, pity or amusement—but a title of tremendous importance, of earth-rocking, heaven-shaking seriousness.

Despite persecution, suffering, even tragedy, gay men and women continue to endure, to hope, to rise again and to make festival—showing us all that life has a meaning if we are foolish enough to believe in it, like Don Quixote. But if gays are clown-figures, clowns are no less Christ-figures. And the Christian meaning of being gay is to that degree made accessible in grasping the point of clowning.

Clowns liberate us from the tedium of the world's grind; they break down the walls of consciousness, which (we thus discover) are mere paper painted to look like bricks. . . . They hold mirrors before us, not of glass but of action, parodying our even more preposterous poses and posturings, our efforts to seem grave and forbidding as we intimidate our nervous way through life. They raise our levels of insight by displacing our dull and customary viewpoint, so that the incongruity and comedy of life are revealed to us with all the fireworks of Sinai. And here again, in the still, small voice heard in the brief pauses between applause and gasps, we detect divine laughter—even in the faint accents of a duck named Donald or an insufficiently suppressed giggle.

In clowns, we, too, "shoot adown titanic glooms of chasméd fears"—to land in a ludicrous heap. But we rise again, shaken but undaunted and start all over again. And we recognize in clowns the divine clown who, his face caked with the white clay of mourning, his painted tears expressing infinite compassion, yet smiling hugely under the vast grin, will forever rise victorious.

And thus the clowns, the gay clowns of the sexual world who bring all men and women again and again to the revelation, the *re-valuation* of the meaning of sexuality and friendship, of hope and the persistent righting of wrongs, find something of their destiny in celebrating and thus overcoming their misfittingness, their outcastness. And in this, because they are not fundamentally alien, they bring humanity to itself.

POSTLUDE

While not a technical treatment, several references to other sources figured throughout this essay, and I wish here to include a few further items: some suggestions for additional reading and a few addresses of organizations serving the gay community.

1. On Sexuality and Homosexuality

Jack Babuscio, *We Speak for Ourselves,* Philadelphia: Fortress Press, 1977.

Gregory Baum, "Catholic Homosexuals," *Commonweal,* 99 (1974), 479–482 (in *Theological/Pastoral Resources*—hereafter *T/P R;* see below).

Howard Brown, *Familiar Faces, Hidden Lives,* New York: Harcourt Brace Jovanovich (Harvest HBJ Book), 1977.

Rita Mae Brown, *Rubyfruit Jungle,* New York: Bantam Books, 1977.

Ronald M. Enroth and Gerald E. Jamison, *The Gay Church,* Grand Rapids, Mich.: William B. Eerdmans Pub. Co., 1974.

Peter Fink, S.J., "Homosexuality, a Pastoral Hypothesis," *Commonweal* (April 6, 1973), 107–112 (in *T/P R*).

Mark Freedman, *Homosexuality and Psychological Functioning,* Belmont, Ca.: Brooks/Cole Pub. Co., 1971.

Don Goergen, *The Sexual Celibate,* New York: Seabury, 1974.

Jeannine Gramick et al., *Homosexual Catholics—A Primer for Discussion,* Boston: Dignity, 1975.

Martin Hoffman, *The Gay World,* New York: Bantam Books, 1969.

Christopher Isherwood, *Christopher and His Kind,* New York: Farrar, Straus & Giroux, 1976.

Eugene Kennedy, *The New Sexuality,* Garden City, N.Y.: Image Books, 1973.

Anthony Kosnik et al., *Human Sexuality: New Directions in American Catholic Thought,* New York: Paulist Press, 1977.

W. D. Oberholtzer, ed., *Is Gay Good?* Philadelphia: The Westminster Press, 1971.

Norman Pittinger, *Time for Consent,* London: SCM Press, 1970.

John Reid, *The Best Little Boy in the World,* New York: Ballantine Books, 1976.

Jane Rule, *Lesbian Images,* New York: Pocket Books, 1976.

Dennis Sanders, *Gay Source: A Catalog for Men,* New York: Coward, McCann & Geoghegan, 1977.

Charles Silverstein, *A Family Matter: A Parents' Guide to Homosexuality,* New York: McGraw-Hill, 1977.

Theological/Pastoral Resources, 4th ed., Oct. 1976, Boston: Dignity (a collection of important articles on homosexuality and religion).

C. V. Tripp, *The Homosexual Matrix,* New York: Signet, 1977.

George Weinberg, *Society and the Healthy Homosexual,* Garden City, N.Y.: Doubleday Anchor Books, 1973.

Ralph W. Weltge, ed., *The Same Sex,* Philadelphia: Pilgrim Press, 1969.

2. On Spirituality, Prophecy and Clowns

Matthew Fox, *Whee! We Wee All the Way Home . . . A Guide to the New Sensual Spirituality,* Wilmington, North Carolina: Consortium Books, 1976.

Joseph C. McLelland, *The Clown and the Crocodile,* Richmond: John Knox Press, 1970.

Milton Mayeroff, *On Caring,* New York: Perennial Library, 1972.

Josef Pieper, *In Tune with the World,* New York: Harcourt, Brace and World, 1965.

Aelred Watkin, *The Enemies of Love,* New York: Paulist Press, 1965.

Enid Welsford, *The Fool: His Social and Literary History,*
  Gloucester, Mass.: Peter Smith, 1966.

3. Addresses (national locations)
Daughters of Bilitis
Room 208
1000 Market Street
San Francisco, California 94103

Dignity, International Office
3719 Sixth Avenue
Suite F
San Diego, California 92103

Integrity, Inc.
5014 Willows Ave.
Philadelphia, Pennsylvania 19143

Lutherans Concerned for Gay People
Box 19114A
Los Angeles, California 90019

Mattachine Society, Inc.
348 Ellis Street
San Francisco, California 94102

Metropolitan Community Church
1050 S. Hill St.
Los Angeles, California 90015

National Gay Task Force
Room 506
80 Fifth Ave.
New York, New York 10011

One, Inc.
2256 Venice Blvd.
Los Angeles, California 90006

Salvatorian Gay Ministry Task Force
1735 Hi-Mount Blvd.
Milwaukee, Wisconsin 53208

OTHER IMAGE BOOKS

OTHER IMAGE BOOKS

OTHER IMAGE BOOKS

OTHER IMAGE BOOKS

A 78 – 4

OTHER IMAGE BOOKS

A 78 – 5